the best of ITALY

vmb
PUBLISHERS

the best of ITALY

CONTENTS

EDITORIAL DIRECTOR
Valeria Manferto De Fabianis

GRAPHIC DESIGN
Anna Galliani
Patrizia Balocco

2-3 Trevi Fountain (1732-1763).

4-5 Venice displays its deeply iridescent nature under different kinds of light, but by night, under the pale glow of the street lamps, the Doge's Palace is profoundly disquieting, as all the phantoms of its glorious past seem to be awakened.

vmb
Published in the USA by
VMB Publishers®
An imprint of White Star, Italy

THE BEST OF ITALY
© 2004 White Star S.r.l.
Via Candido Sassone, 22/24
13100 Vercelli, Italy
www.whitestar.it

ISBN 88-540-0110-4

REPRINTS:
1 2 3 4 5 6 08 07 06 05 04

Printed in China

6 Ponte (Bridge) Vittorio Emanuele II with Gianicolo (Janiculum) Hill in the background.

7 The title of the fountain by Bartolomeo Ammannati in Piazza della Signoria in Florence is **Neptune's Chariot.** *But the Florentines all know it as* il Biancone.

Taken from:

ROME
Impressions, recollections and charm
© 1995, 1999 White Star S.r.l.
ISBN 88-8095-343-5

VENETO
An enchanting paradise of art
© 2002 White Star S.r.l.
ISBN 88-8095-775-9

TUSCANY
The horizons of art and beauty
© 1995 White Star S.r.l.
ISBN 88-8095-777-5

SICILY
A Meeting of Mediterranean Civilizations
© 2002 White Star S.r.l.
ISBN 88-8095-776-7

INTRODUCTION

Whenever we hear a country mentioned, some defining characteristic immediately comes to mind.

It may be something we have read or seen illustrated or, if we know the country through a visit or vacation, it may be a particular city square, cathedral or monument, a notable mountain range or landscape, an historical event or perhaps an historically rich local festival or custom.

As the world is filled with magnificent vistas, great cities, and masterpieces of art, what rises up in memory or imagination is practically limitless.

When we think of Italy – leaving aside the clichés – what will probably come to mind is exuberant creativity, incarnated in glorious "art cities" or perhaps the ever-varied, nature-blessed landscapes of a country that from its northern mountains

and lakes to its southern "boot" boldly divides the Mediterranean and its hinterlands.

The range of appropriate "attributes" at hand in attempting to "define" Italy is so wide as to be embarrassing. What, then, is Italy? What do we feel when we hear its name? The fullness and resonance of an answer of course depends on our knowledge, experience and understanding of Italy, on how we can integrate the peninsula's history, scenery, people, culture and customs into a manageable whole.

This volume attempts the impossible: to capture and present in narrative and illustration the "best" of Italy and to provide a tribute to all that this treasure house of landscapes, cities, and art offers to the world.

8-9 Piazza dei Miracoli with the Duomo, the Baptistery, and the Tower, Pisa.

9 Via Conciliazione and St. Peter's Basilica (1506-1614), Rome.

Rome, once a great empire's "Capital of the World" and long "The Eternal City" is at Italy's center, an inexhaustible realm of history, architecture and art, but nonetheless only part of the larger whole. To the northeast are the prosperous cities and farmlands of the Veneto region, with its unique jewel of Venice (how many of the world's loveliest canal-quartered cities have poetically termed themselves "the Venice of ...")?). In the distant sun-drenched south, Sicily rises from the sea, its deep-layered Graeco-Roman-Arabic-Norman-Spanish history and pulsing warmth and sensuality rendering it an island world apart,

Then there is the heartland of Tuscany with its unrivaled capital of Florence, haven and heaven to generations of European and American travelers in search of history, landscape, and all the joys of life. Epitome and paradigm of so much beauty, Tuscany (the land of the Tusci, the mysterious Etruscans) is the cradle of the Renaissance, home to marvelous works of art and nature, the region where Leonardo da Vinci is only one of a myriad of artists, architects, sculptors and men of learning. This volume and the four regions it presents offer an unmatched portrait of Italy.

The "best" can never be "all of the best,"

and our hope is that this selection will enrich memory for those who know Italy and open the doors of curiosity to those that do not yet know her. We hope also that it will lead to the exploration of Italy's many other fabled regions of historic cities, noble castles, art-rich cathedrals and ways of life so spontaneous, vibrant and rewarding that once known live on in memory.

12-13 The silhouettes of cypresses, symbols of the Sienese countryside, emerge out of the morning mist near Asciano.

14-15 Tindari: salt lakes formed by the sand.

16 *The Pantheon Fountain (1575), Piazza della Rotonda.*

18-19 *The Fontana dei Fiumi, or Fountain of the Four Rivers, (1650-1651), Piazza Navona.*

impressions, recollections and charm

ROME

impressions, recollections and charm

ROME

CONTENTS

21 Statue of the Angel with the Crown of Thorns (1667-1669), Ponte Sant'Angelo.

22-23 The Colosseum (72-82 A.D.).

24-25 Castel Sant'Angelo (140 A.D.) was rebuilt in the sixteenth century.

IN·AERVMNA·MEA
DVM·CONFIGITVR·SPINA

INTRODUCTION

Eternal Rome. Sacred Rome. Secular Rome. Aristocratic and arrogant, ancient and modern, rhetorical and opulent and yet minimalist, Rome is the city of little things, of hidden corners, of breathtaking colors in a chanced upon dawn or blood red sunset. It is hard to find words that will not seem exaggerated. The best way is to look through the cold eyes of the reporter, and undoubtedly, through those of History. Mysterious and inscrutable, Rome is a truly unique city. It has inspired poets, painters, and great artists of all times. It has always been an obligatory point of passage in the evolution of numerous cultures, yet it has lost none of its spontaneity. Its inhabitants are sociable as nowhere else and will reserve a warm welcome for all, right down to the last of the occasional tourists.

Those visiting once, those passing through, and even those arriving on vacation all know from the very first that they will return. Rome is not easily forgotten. You will know it by its colors, its smells, its noises, even blindfolded. The perpetual charm prevails over the chaos, the smog, the disorganization, the noise, and the construction frauds that have fuelled controversy and discontent over the Rome of the twenty-first century. Unequalled anywhere in the world for its works of art, it is, first and foremost, ancient Rome. The sense of majesty in its monuments struck the great artist Giorgio De Chirico profoundly. After a brief period of study in the capital, he wrote that "In Rome the sense of prophecy is more extensive. A sensation of infinite and distant greatness.

26-27 A sweeping view of the Aventine Hill.

The same as that impressed by the Roman mason upon the arch, the reflection of that awe of the infinite which the celestial stratum sometimes produces in man." From white marble it has drawn the mark of immortality. The Mamertine prison, the ancient Cloaca Massima, and the Servian walls, which from the mid fourth century B.C. marked the confines of the city and saved it from Hannibal's horde, have all stood the test of time. The golden quadrangle of archaeology, a mine of information for researchers of all times, is still there circumscribed by the Palatine, Campidoglio, Viminal, and Quirinal despite the the asphalt strip called Via dei Fori Imperiali imposed by Mussolini during the years of fascism which cut the quadrangle in two. Inside the Roman Forum, the heart of the Roman Republic, are the remains of the ancient Curia, the Arch of Septimus Severus, the ruins of the temples of Saturn and the statues of the dioscuri, the temple of Antonino and Faustina, the House of the Vestal Virgins and, lastly, the splendid Arch of Titus. The Imperial Forum complex contains the Colosseum and the remains of Trajan's Markets and Column.

The eye is lost in a maze of marble, here and there concealed by tufts of nettles. Wily cats, the true masters of ancient Rome, doze in opulence amid the House of Livia, the Domus Augustana, and the Thermae. The Palatine is considered the lap of Rome: in the times of the Emperors it was the heart of the

28-29 Piazza del Campidoglio (sixteenth century).

29 One of the dioscuri, Piazza del Campidoglio (first century B.C.-third century A.D.).

city. On the Capitoline hill stood the temple of Jupiter, a fragment of ancient memories gone for ever. These re-emerge in the fourteenth century image of Petrarch crowned as a poet, or in the perfect geometrical lines of Michelangelo, who redesigned the Piazza del Campidoglio, initialing the paving. Passing today on those ancient stones are the Mayor and the Aldermen, as well as newly-wed couples for whom a photo with the Campidoglio as a backdrop or beside the long stairway of Ara Coeli is a must. Even Bill and Hillary – Clinton, of course - posed amid the ancient Capitoline ruins during their celebrated Italian holiday, she smiling, dressed in fiery red, and he moved by the memories and charm of the ancient setting. In the sixteenth century Rome enjoyed its second youth with the arrival of Bramante, Bernini, Borromini, Michelangelo, and Raphael. After centuries of darkness, the city began to put on a fresh face as new structures such as Palazzo Farnese, the Quirinal, Villa Medici, and Porta Pia by Michelangelo were erected as well as churches, the sacred soul of Rome.

This soul was also bound to tradition and culture through opera with that famous encounter in Sant'Andrea della Valle between Tosca and Cavaradossi. While sighs and murmurs seem to echo among the marble of the ancient church, the opera becomes life, reawakened by the aromas of the nearby restaurants, their names still celebrating Puccini's heroine in this city looking towards the third millenium. Sacred Rome offers the churches, the Pope and St Peter's Basilica with its Cupola, the Basilica of Santa Maria degli Angeli and that of St.s Peter and Paul. Sights and sensations include the smell of incense, floors polished by invisible attendants, and the passing of nimble altar boys. The ray of light piercing St Peter's from on high, like the withering eye of God, brings no feelings of fear. Those looking up towards the smallest ring of the dome are more likely to be dazzled. The imagination will race back in time to the works planned by Bramante and carried out by Giuliano da Sangallo, then Raphael, Peruzzi, Sangallo again and, lastly, by Michelangelo with his special touch. There is the Dome, the colonnade, the Loggia, Raphael's rooms, and the final triumph of the Sistine Chapel. Oddly enough, it took the Japanese and their sponsorship to lift the haze of ancient patina and return the colors to their splendor as created by Michelangelo. However, this is part of the good and the bad of Rome: it is the home of the Romans but its offspring are citizens of the world.

Once upon a time for the populace of sacred and papal Rome the great Basilica was but a place of worship.

30 Interior of the Basilica
di San Paolo fuori le Mura
(fourth-ninth centuries
A.D.). Saint Paul Outside
the Walls was rebuilt in
1854.

30-31 The statue of Rome
(1471), Piazza del
Campiáoglio.

*32-33 The statue of the
Angel with the Lance
and Castel Sant'Angelo.*

*33 Detail of Ponte
Sant'Angelo, or Sant'Angelo
Bridge, (second century
A.D.) with the castle in the
background.*

It was not the city of the Pope but the burial place of Peter, founder of the Catholic Church. The Borgo district soon took on an international air. Representing the heart and soul of St Peter's, its name comes from the German burg, a German matrix for a mesh of streets and alleys untouched by time and, in some corners, by light too. The Borgo streets are part of the appeal and heart of papal Rome. Passing through them today one is unaware of all the history in these narrow little streets.

Today the shop windows glitter with holy souvenirs. Miniatures of the Basilica are flanked by portable replicas of the Pietà, glass domes contain the Cupola in a snow storm, and t-shirts bear the Pope's image. To think that in the times of Boniface VIII and the great invention of the Jubilee, Borgo was the Christian soul of the city and the expression of the impervious road to Heaven, symbolized at the end of the darkness by the shaft of light and the silhouette of the great dome.

With St. Peter's as Heaven, Peter's tomb represents the highest and mightiest symbol of the city of God. Built up haphazardly and then hewn down by the urban renewal which destroyed it, the Borgo district has nonetheless maintained its "color." Small shops line narrow streets where the buildings huddle together, including the barber shop, the old cobbler, the tailor, the bakery with the fragrant smell of bread cooked in a wood oven, the pizza place with its old sign, the old grocery stores, and the chair-weavers.

Strangely enough, all this has just as much to do with holy Rome as the black habits dotting the white square which conjure up the seventeenth century's black costumes and wall hangings, representing the color of mourning and the Inquisition. Two dates reawaken in the Romans the mysteries and secrets of the temporal power of the Church.

On September 11, 1599, Beatrice Cenci, victim of a family tragedy now a legend in Rome, was punished, and on February 17, 1600, Giordano Bruno was burned at the stake.

Today, Monte Cenci smells of traditional Roman fritti and carciofi alla giudìa, while in Piazza Farnese, shoppers at the oldest and most popular market of the city jostle around the block commemorating Giordano Bruno.

Secular Rome can be found in the villas, gardens, and the carnival celebrations in baroque Piazza Navona. Further back in history, gladiators fought in the Colosseum and blood ran over the travertine of the Flavian Amphitheater as the fighters of Ancient Rome entered the arena to amuse the Emperor. Chosen from among prisoners of war, criminals, slaves, and volunteers, they were destined to die and fought for the delight of the public.

Only the mercy or a whim of the Emperor could save their lives. Secular Rome could also be cruel at times. There was the crazy Rome of Nero's follies and the magnificent Rome of the baroque Carnevale, with Piazza Navona flooded to become a pool.

Rome has its records and history, its curiosities and legends such as the time when at the end of the seventeenth century a poetry presentation on the Campidoglio sought the enchantment of Olympia. For the Arcadian poets Rome was to be the new paradise, an Olympus of secularity and poetry under the banner of Pan and his pipes. The Campidoglio was transformed into a bucolic rendez-vous and the poets sought new life in the breath of secular Rome.

Thinking back, the atmosphere must have been like that of an ephemeral Roman summer ante litteram with free verse in the spirit of the pastoral world. Shepherds and inspiring nymphs would be found where Roman senators had stood, while Greek-style tunics would have fluttered in the place of the purple-edged laticlavium of the Imperial senators.

A truly profane rejoicing, the Arcadia marked its days with hedonistic love affairs. However, intermediary love poems and literary mediocrity soon lost momentum.

34-35 *The Obelisk of Santa Maria sopra Minerva, Piazza della Minerva (sixth century A.D.).*

36-37 *The Steps of Trinità dei Monti (1724-1726).*

38-39 Piazza Navona.

Passing through Rome, Carlo Goldoni, with a hint of superiority, branded the ancien regime culture of Arcadia in his Memoires, caustically ridiculing Sybil and the oracles decorated with drooping laurel..

The romantic strolls of the poets on their cultural travels were characteristic of secular Rome.

Keats, Byron, and Shelley, along with Stendhal's "Les Promenades dans Rome," Goethe's "Italian Journey," and the secret, scandalous itineraries of Roger Peyrefitte were followed by contemporary writers such as Truman Capote, Gore Vidal.

One place that conjures up the artists and Bohemia of this aspect of Rome is the ancient Cafè Greco, just one step away from Piazza di Spagna, two from the stairway, three from Via del Corso, and four from Via del Babuino.

Now, the cups with the gold and bright orange stripe are sold as souvenirs, but the worn marble tables and the slightly misshapen floor reveal more sumptuous times. No mention is made of forbidden love affairs, surreptitious encounters, passionate betrayals, and agonizing platonic loves.

Oscar Wilde came often to Italy. He lived in Rome and extolled it after his stay in 1877. His verses, inspired by Shelley, Byron, and Keats, who had all preceded him in the Italian pilgrimage, perfectly convey the romanticism and pagan glorification of the Rome fantasized about by the English poets.

The author of Salome wrote odes to the tombs of Shelley and Keats. Reading those verses, the profane grandeur of this romantic city sends the imagination racing to that red house on Piazza di Spagna where the poet lived, and to the colors, the noises, the creaking of the last carriages on the stones of Piazza di Spagna, and the wan light of the sunset when the stairway lit up with stars, as opposed to the neon signs now coldly indicating the entrance to fast food eating places, or the underground which every fifteen minutes from beneath the steps of Trinità dei Monti vomits hordes of tourists, more interested in a pair of jeans than in lost sentiment.

The poetry of that unique staircase will not, nonetheless, die. It will endure the crowds of springtime tourists which turn the travertine streets worn by centuries of passing feet into an anthill of upturned heads, all gazing at Villa Medici. It will likewise endure the onset of summer, when it becomes a catwalk in honor of high fashion as Valentino and Armani sit in the front row and, together with the stars of international show business, applaud Claudia Schiffer and Naomi Campbell.

On that night the splendor of the stairway disappears as if by magic and the fascination of Piazza di Spagna fades in the evanescent light of a luxury fashion show.

Yet, when the spotlights go off, Trinità dei Monti becomes itself again, the intense pink and bright red of its azaleas like fireworks lighting up the white travertine. Meanwhile, the guitars and flutes of the odd eccentric tourist will accompany his search for lost coins here and there amid the fluttering ribbon of people climbing and descending to the silver blade of Via Condotti, historically the most fashionable street facing the steps.

This is the heart of luxury shopping and "Made in Italy" style, where the wealthiest tourists are attracted by designer labels such as Bulgari, Giorgio Armani, Prada, Ferragamo, and Battistoni.

The words of the poet Alfonso Gatto say much about the atmosphere of secular Rome between the two wars: "I had just arrived in Rome from Salerno and I was still dazed. My poet friend, older than I, said, 'This evening I'll show you the king of Rome.'

'Who is it?' 'Scipione!' We went all over.

To Aragno's, Piazza del Popolo, Piazza Navona. Nothing. Not a trace of this Scipione. It was almost daylight and we were about to return home, cold and disappointed, when on Gianicolo Hill we saw a bonfire and a crowd of people shouting excitedly. There were half-dressed whores and, at the center, there he was making obscene gestures illuminated by the firelight. I, who had come from Salerno, asked my friend 'Where have you brought me?.'"

Scipione is one of few contemporary artists to have grasped the intoxification of "pagan" Rome.

He is especially sensitive to its colors like the reddish glare of some of the façades in Piazza Navona and the blinding white of the statues which seems to bring them to life, making them speak and palpitate.

Rome can also be arrogant with its noble palaces and the power that lurks in Montecitorio or the Vatican. Federico Fellini lived a stone's throw from Piazza del Popolo, and his home became a rendez-vous for the film world, politicians, journalists, and high society. He understood this aspect of Rome so well that he presented it with the most cruelly honest portraits of its shortcomings in Roma, Satyricon, and La Dolce Vita.

In 1960, while the intelligentsia was meeting at the fashionable Café de Paris and Doney's, Via Veneto

40 top The courtyard of San Silvestro (eighth century A.D.).

40 bottom Piazza dei Mercanti, Trastevere.

40-41 The Arco degli Acetati, between Pellegrino Street and Campo de' Fiori.

was the fulcrum of high society life. Here were the friends of Pannunzio's Il Mondo, as well as any film stars passing through. Rome was becoming a philosophy, a way of life, no longer a mere city. Bustling away, Rome became a great setting for the artists who immortalized its suburbs, substance, color, lifestyle, and its very spirit. It was transformed into a set destined to make a permanent mark on the history of Italian theatre, as well as that of the great Hollywood film world. The fairy tale of "Hollywood on the Tiber" was born as paparazzi, high society, and vacant cocktail parties catered to the public relations of the stars. In Via Veneto a famous restaurant where Richard Burton wooed Liz Taylor still conserves mementoes of their passage through Rome. Gossip and scandals soon followed. The city was the backdrop and its Sixties were colored with romance.

Rome's arrogance, cinematographical in this case, snowballed. Great actors, great films, great investments in celluloid, and legendary grandeur in the studios welcomed for the first time the smell of greenbacks and the great names from Los Angeles.

Luxury restaurants and glittering hotels were the stage for the caprices of the stars. Fellini and Flaiano did not invent a character like Marcello in "La Dolce Vita" by chance. That fashionable and vain segment of the Rome that had won over the hearts of foreigners, and of Hollywood, really existed. It was an ongoing exhibition of vanity, grown out of the ruins of neo-realistic Rome as immortalized by Roberto Rossellini. The rhythm really was like that of the transient cardboard set. As 1959 was coming to a close and "La Dolce Vita" was about to launch Via Veneto as a must for wealthy high society the world over, Flaiano, speaking about the atmosphere in Rome the morning after the follies and caprices of the nocturnal jet set, said, "the air was clear then, the traffic quiet, and from the baker's shop wafted the smell of hot croissants. There was a jolly, small town bustle, journalists and writers were having a drink before lunch, the painters had no dealers, and people did not take planes much...."

Today Via Veneto is regular location for events.

Every film or society occasion is an excuse to rekindle memories or tune in to the waves of revival. Doney's, the Café de Paris, and Harry's Bar have resisted.

Unfortunately, the old bakery smelling of fresh bread has been suffocated by banks. The ritual of the intellectual aperitif has faded with time, lost in the rapid consumption of a quick sandwich or the business brunch of the street's new inhabitants. Those white collars with their gray jackets and regimental ties regularly step out with their mobile phones in their pockets, ready to fly off. It is difficult, or rather impossible, to restore the Via Veneto of the past and to bring "La Dolce Vita" back to life thirty years later. Valentino, fashion designer par excellence and dressmaker to the great ladies of the world, tried for fun to revive the splendid image of "La Dolce Vita" of the past by bringing a new Anita Ekberg to Trevi Fountain. But can a Claudia Schiffer embody the charm and opulence of Fellini's star of the Sixties? In Rome, the magic of that period was nearly rediscovered for one night. Rome is a rhetorical, aulic, and imposing city with great palaces where the strategies of power are decided. It is a city of ritual appointments. One is the Pope's Angelus every Sunday at noon in Piazza San Pietro. There is always a crowd of applauding believers, although in recent years there has also been a host of rolling TV cameras carrying the Pope's message and blessing to the whole universe of followers tuned in at home. The square starts to fill from the early hours of the morning with hordes of tourists and buses filled with chattering pilgrims from near and far. A multicolored mass of appreciative men and women raise their eyes to the Pope's window asking for a glance, a word, or just a nod of the head.

44 The Temple of Vesta (second century B.C.), Piazza Bocca della Verità.

44-45 The Temple of Aesculapius (eighteenth century A.D.), Villa Borghese gardens.

46-47 Fontana dei Fiumi
(1650-1651), Piazza Navona.

48-49 A carriage in
St Peter's Square.

Another rapt and applauding crowd can be found at the Quirinal for the changing of the guard.

On the other hand, there is the annual rhetoric of the Roman Christmas, a street festival which continues to offer its lights and colorful markets selling cheap dreams in baroque Piazza Navona. While the consumer rites of shoppers are celebrated in the golden streets of the old city center, the lights of Piazza Navona come on in anticipation of the Epiphany. For the Romans, Piazza Navona is the home of the friendly old hag of the Epiphany and where one can, now at great expense, purchase gifts for the traditional stocking as well as the latest handmade Nativity scenes made by craftsmen from Naples with little statues made of the traditional papier-mâché and colored chalk of the Christmas mangers of yesteryear in defiance of today's plastic ones. Rhetorical Rome preserves its traditions. On Sunday mornings in the Pincio gardens with the swans' on the lake, the pony and cart await smiling children. On Gianicolo (Janiculum) Hill, Rome still renders homage to Garibaldi, but the midday canon blast is now deadened by horns and droning engines. Only in the Pincio gardens of Rome, every Sunday morning, the puppet show is repeated for the youngest spectators. Punch has had the same voice for forty, perhaps fifty, years. It is now recorded and transmitted to preserve the charm, but once upon a time the slightly nasal tones were heard live every week as the live applause of the small crowd of onlookers greeted their hero.

Rome is also the city of mothers and children, and of wives and girlfriends. It is famous for stolen kisses before the loveliest panorama of the city, sighs captured among the stately busts in the Pincio gardens, or slightly over-audacious caresses in the dark while descending from the great terrace to Villa Medici and then further down to the stairway of Piazza di Spagna.

In the times of Shelley and Keats, rhetorical Rome was heard in the sound of a carriage on the cobbles. More recently, it was the guitar of some hippy passing through or a crackling pan of chestnuts at the foot of the Spanish steps. Yesterday the chestnut sellers were Romans, their cheeks burned by the first of the north winds.

Today, at even the most inconvenient hours, the grills are subcontracted out, perhaps to some north African who has already learnt all he needs to know from the dying breed of chestnut-sellers, such as how to make more money by not completely filling the shriveled paper cone. Minimalist Rome is also an everyday city. It is anything but the city of legend and courtly poems.

Contemporary Rome consists of real life, everyday noises, mopeds darting away at green lights, road sweepers in action, and restaurants smelling of spring lamb and meatballs, ribbon pasta and fried dishes, spaghetti with tomato and basil sauce with a mountain of Parmesan cheese sprinkled over it, and meat as red as the sunsets over the Pincio hill. The noise of the traffic fails to totally cover the sounds of the traditional crafts. It seems incredible but on some days, in some places and streets, the musical lament of the knife-grinder seeking knives to sharpen and the refrain of the umbrella-mender who changes the ribs of broken umbrellas still rise above the din of engines and televisions. TV aerials tower above ancient palaces, satellite dishes appear on the terraces of the "better" districts, but the voice of the old craftsmen can still be heard. It is not an issue if the knife-grinder now uses a motor instead of bicycle pedals to turn his stone, or if the umbrella-mender uses better tools than in times gone by.

The Rome of today, with a few too many fast food restaurants and large suburban stores, is living on interest from its past, cultivating its own philosophy of life. In art, this minimalist, commonplace Rome harks back to Mafai's taverns, Vittorio De Sica's neo-realistic bicycles, the visionary and sanguinary city of Scipione, the ideal Rome of Siron, and to the black and white Rome of Pasolini's decadence in the films Mamma Roma and Accattone.

Rome is a city of fiery moods and strong tones, of unique color and magic light. Famous photographers

and leading film directors are well aware of the importance of catching a color, a frame, or an image of Rome at the right moment. Rome will awaken and suddenly come alive as the hearts of its statues seem to revive. The sun turns the contours of the dioscuri pink, then golden, blood red, and brown.

The night sky silhouettes the unmistakable outline of the Colosseum and illuminates the whiteness of the Pincio with pale moonlight. One and only Rome is proud and sensual, a little haughty in the sunlight, silvery and pale when the moon comes out, veiled

with mist when the southeast wind delays the rising
sun, and somber and gray when the sky unexpectedly
clouds over and rain pours menacingly on the ancient
marbles and baroque lines of the great statues.

The magic moment is at sunset, when the red
houses light up with tones as warm as the burning
sun. This is the hour of the artists, poets, and
photographers, when the last boatmen plough across
the tawny Tiber River. For visitors, it is an
enchanting moment that generates sensations and
feelings unique to Rome.

50-51 and 52-53
Ai Cinecittà, the plaster
statue storeroom.

Everything lights up only to dim in the Roman twilight before the night comes alive. At this point in the day, Rome shows its other face, black as ink but alive with inimitable fragrances such as the mint growing wild amid the ruins of the Forum, or the perfume of the last oranges left battling against the concrete on the Aventine Hill. The citrus trees may be a little wild but they are as ancient as the gardens they belong to, from where they gaze beyond the Tiber to where the minimalist Rome of the last surviving craftsmen and that somewhat exaggeratedly folkloristic neighborhood Trastevere (made so for foreign tourists) indulge in the last, daily rituals of the popular and wily city which grew up in the shadow of the Pope-King.

54 The sacred area (third-first centuries B.C.), Largo di Torre Argentina.

55 The Temple of Apollo Sosiano (fourth-first century B.C.). The Synagogue (1904) can be seen in the background.

56-57 The Imperial Forum (second-first centuries B.C.).

58-59 Statues on Ponte Vittorio Emanuele II, with the dome of St. Peter's in the background.

*60 and 61 Details of statues
in the Fontana dei Fiumi
(1650-1651), Piazza Navona.*

A STUNNING BEAUTY

"Without having seen Rome one cannot rightly imagine the effect it can have. It seems a city observed through a glass which magnifies its contours. One would say that the houses, the squares, the churches, the fountains, the steps, the columns, and all the monuments in Rome were created by a race of men physically twice our size. One must crane one's neck to see the tops of the buildings and columns.

One needs a telescope to see the end of the squares and a carriage to move about. As a city it is astounding – that is the right word. The first instinct felt is the need to have someone alongside and to clutch his arm so tight as to bruise him. Were it not for the people all around one would cry out."

Edmondo De Amicis,
"Ricordi di Roma," from
Ricordi del 1870-1871,
Florence: Barbera, 1873.

"J'AI PLUS DE SOUVENIR QUE SI J'AVAIS MILLE ANS"

"To speak of Rome is for me a sweet but serious task. Sweet because no subject attracts me or gratifies me more. Serious not just because Rome is Rome, but rather because I have lived in this city for more than a quarter of a century and I could use Baudelaire's words to say of it, 'J'ai plus de souvenirs que si j'avais mille ans.' I have seen the waiters of the Café Aragno grow old, the women I have loved or liked in youth fade, many illusions and many friendships go to ruin, but Rome has been transformed, rejuvenated, and has grown year by year, with no mercy for our personal attachments and melancholies. Oh no, Rome is no easy city, no kind city!"

VINCENZO CARDARELLI,
CIELO SULLE CITTÀ,
MILAN: BOMPIANI, 1939.

62 Columns of the Temple of Apollo Sosiano (fourth-first centuries B.C.). In the background, the Teatro Marcello (first century B.C. - fourth century A.D.).

63 The Arch of Septimus Severus (second century A.D.), Roman Forum.

TO ROME, THE ETERNAL CITY

"Eternal spirit, eternal courage, oh Rome! After all the blood, after a long period of oblivion, the raging thunder and the feeble silence, so many downfalls and so many flames lit by all the winds, you with your own feet treading on your ashes, your ruins ever higher, you celebrate the greatest of your triumphs, that you have beaten death. You before all the peoples that you called to be rightly yours, now you appear again in the first flower of youth, extraordinary, like Pallante, defended all around by glittering weapons and with the sword; and hanging above the world that light with which lit the peoples all their light, that which breaks our obscurity. Oh mighty Rome, the mighty yours more than time the lamp of life."

GIOVANNI PASCOLI,
POEMI DEL RISORGIMENTO,
BOLOGNA: ZANICHELLI, 1913.

A GLANCE, AN EMBRACE...

68 *Panoramic view with the Altare della Patria (1885-1911) in the background.*

69 *Sacred area (third-first century B.C.), Largo di Torre Argentina.*

"Looking down, from the roof of the church to where you have just been, you will see a procession of ants. You can only just make out the people strolling in the square, the two large fountains seem two quivering white plumes, and the smaller domes of the Basilica those little bells used for the statues of saints. All the city is embraced at a glance. The first thing you notice are the walls of the Colosseum and the Thermae, huge and black. The statues on the top of the columns, the tips of the obelisks, the curving banks of the Tiber, Pincio hill, Villa Borghese, the Quirinal, San Giovanni Laterano, Gianicolo, looking like a little hill in a garden, all can be seen clearly. The Vatican garden seems a flower bed, the Vatican a nondescript building, with little courtyards; al! is closed and deserted. There is Monte Mario. And down there the Roman countryside, sinister and bare; from here they must have seen the divisions of the Cadorna passing, company after company, canon after canon. Monterotondo, Tivoli, Frascati, Albano and, farther right, in the distance, that thin line glittering, the sea. Rome! Rome! A blessed name one never tires of uttering; there is a secret somewhere in this sound: Rome! It seems to continue echoing in the ear: Rome! Here it all is...."

EDMONDO DE AMICIS,
"RICORDI DI ROMA," FROM
RICORDI DEL 1870-1871,
FLORENCE: BARBERA, 1873.

*70 top Carabinieri
(policemen) on horseback in
the Imperial Forums.*

*70 bottom Detail of the
fountain in front of the
National Roman Museum.*

*70-71 A park near the
Imperial Forums.*

72 Carriages in Piazza
di Spagna.

73 The Columns of the
Temple of Adrian (145
A.D.), today the stock
exchange, Piazza di Pietra:

74-75 Trastevere, the steps
of Viale Glorioso.

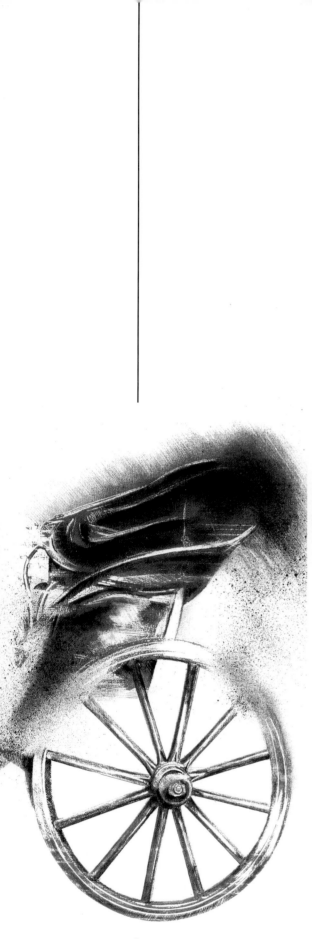

76-77 Carriages in Piazza di Spagna.

GENTLE BAROQUE WATERS

"A great silence, broken only by the sound of falling water…Sylvia comes upon a small deserted square, one wall taken over by an enormous baroque fountain, all statues, decorations, the roar of water. Enchanted, Sylvia gazes at the unreal beauty of the scene…."

FROM THE ORIGINAL SCREENPLAY OF *LA DOLCE VITA*, FEDERICO FELLINI, PUBLISHED BY CAPPELLI.

78-79 Trevi Fountain (1732-1763).

THE ROMANS? NOTHING WILL SURPRISE THEM

"…The Roman's indifference is a pretence, an ancient pretence come back, not presumption. Flaiano in his An Alien in Rome describes it to perfection: the Roman never marvels at anything. Whoever comes to Rome, it makes no difference to him. He has already seen so much, because he has been around so long and knows he is in one of the loveliest places in the world; there is no question about that.

FROM AN INTERVIEW WITH MONICA VITTI, ITALIAN ACTRESS.

80-81 The Pantheon (first century B.C.).

82-83 The Spanish Steps (1724-1726) and Trinità dei Monti.

DROPLETS OF GLISTENING LIGHT

"What filled me with joy that day was something akin to love – but not love – or at least not that love talked about and sought by men, and not even the sense of beauty. It came not from a woman; nor did it come from my thoughts. I will write and you will understand if I say that it was none other than the mere glorification of Light? I was seated in that garden. I could not see the sun but the air shone with indirect light as if the blue sky had turned to liquid and rained down. Yes, truly, there were ripples, engulfing light. On the musk were flecks like droplets. Yes, truly the light seemed to flow along that wide avenue with golden bubbles left on the branch tips amid the streaming rays."

ANDRÉ GIDE,
LES NOURRITURES TERRESTRES,
PARIS: GALLIMARD, 1942.

84 top The bust of Giovanni Maria Lancisi in the Pincio gardens (eighteenth century) with the pine trees of Villa Borghese in the background.

84 bottom View from Gianicolo Hill. On the right, San Pietro in Montorio (fifteenth century).

84-85 The Aventine Hill. Santa Sabina (fifth century A.D.) with the dome of St. Peter's in the background.

84 top The bust of Giovanni Maria Lancisi in the Pincio gardens (eighteenth century) with the pine trees of Villa Borghese in the background.

84 bottom View from Gianicolo Hill. On the right, San Pietro in Montorio (fifteenth century).

84-85 The Aventine Hill. Santa Sabina (fifth century A.D.) with the dome of St. Peter's in the background.

86-87 Sheep along the Via Appia Antica (Old Appia Way).

87 The characteristic pavement of the Via Appia Antica.

THE PERPETUAL CHARM
OF THE ANCIENT COUNTRYSIDE

"Antiquity does survive in the countryside: fallow, empty, accursed as the desert, with its great stretches of aqueducts and its herds of big-horned cattle. This is truly beautiful, the antique beauty one has imagined."

GUSTAVE FLAUBERT, FROM
A LETTER TO LOUIS BOUILHET,
ROME, APRIL 9, 1851,
THE LETTERS OF 1830-57,
LONDON: FABER & FABER, 1979.

THE TIBER, TAWNY
AND TREACHEROUS

88-89 Ponte Cestio (first century B.C.) and the Isola Tiberina.

"The boatman who ferried me across yesterday to the other side of the Tiber where, beneath the fine leafy trees, the yellow trelliswork of the bathing establishment rises from the tawny water, told me very seriously, 'My dear sir, too many establishments! Too many! Napoli, Livorno, Civitavecchia, Vicarello! Nowadays there are more establishments than bathers. Of course business is bad.'

The "Charon," who for two coins carries bodies and souls from one side of the Tiber to the other and vice versa, is a real river dog: thin but strong, with a white woolly beard which does justice to a face burnt by the sun. He sits solemnly at the stern of one of his boats, called Noah's Ark, leaving his post only to proudly collect the price of the brief river journey in his cap. He has two favorite topics of conversation and they never last longer than the crossing: the explanation of the workings of the pulley, which runs on a taut cord between the two river banks keeping the boat secure, and the description of a journey he made in his youth following the Tiber upstream from Ripetta to Stimigliano. [It was] a voyage of squalls, tempests, choppy water, eddies, vortexes, and turmoil. God save us all, to have made it home again."

CESARE PASCARELLA,
"LE CAMPANE DI RIPETTA,"
PROSE 1880-1890,
TURIN: S.T.E.N., 1920.

90-91 Paola Fontana (1612), Via Garibaldi.

92-93 Ponte Vittorio Emanuele II.

94-95 Detail of a statue (1667-1669), Ponte Sant'Angelo (second century A.D.).

AT SUNRISE, AT SUNSET:
A UNIQUE LIGHT

"Nothing is comparable in beauty to the outline of the Roman horizon, to the gentle slope of the plains, or to the soft, fleeting contours of the mountains confining it. Often in the countryside the valleys take on the form of an arena, a circus, a hippodrome; the flanks of the hills are cut in terraces, as if the mighty hand of the Romans had shifted all that soil. A peculiar haze spread out in the distance fills out the objects masking what might be harsh or brusque in form. The shadows are never heavy and black. There are no masses of rock and scrub so obscure that a little light does not find its way in. A singularly harmonious hue embraces the land, the heavens, the water.

Thanks to imperceptible shades of color all the surfaces blend at their edges, making it impossible to ascertain where one ends and the other commences. You must certainly have admired the landscapes of Claude Lorraine with that light seemingly perfect and lovelier than nature? Well, it is the light of Rome! I never tire of seeing Villa Borghese, or the sun setting on the cypresses of Monte Mario or on the pine trees of Villa Pamphili, planted by Le Notre. Often have I gone up the Tiber to Ponte Molle to delight in the great spectacle of the day's end.

The peaks of the Sabina mountains then seem made of lapis lazuli and pale gold, their bases and flanks steeped in a haze of violet or scarlet.

Sometimes lovely clouds are carried like light chariots on the evening wind with unequalled grace, explaining the apparition of Olympus' inhabitants beneath this mythological sky.

Sometimes Ancient Rome seems to have sent westwards all the purple of its consuls and its Caesars, under the feet of the god of the day.

This rich decoration does not vanish so quickly as in our climes: when you believe the tones are about to die away all springs to life again in some other part of the horizon, one twilight after another, and the magic of the sunset is prolonged. It is true that at this hour of rest for the countryside the air no longer reverberates with bucolic songs. There are no more shepherds: Dulcia linquimus arva! But the great victims of Clitumnus are still to be seen, white oxen and herds of half-wild mares descending the banks of the Tiber, come to drink its waters. You would think yourself taken back to the time of the old Sabines or the century of the Arcadian Evander, when the Tiber was called Albula and the pious Aeneas sailed up its unknown waters."

RÉNÉ F. CHATEAUBRIAND
"LETTRE À M. DE FONTANES
SUR LA CAMPAGNE ROMAINE"
ANTIQUE EDITION FOR
J. M. GAUTIER, LIBRAIRIE
DROZ, GENEVE, LILLE:
LIBRAIRIE GIARD, 1951.

ROME, THE HOME OF POETS

"How often have I fantasized on the steps of Piazza di Spagna, up against Keats' house, caught in the rush of steps like a wheel in that of a watermill! How often have I rode in a carriage around the Colosseum, that vast receptacle of moonlight and dreams, seemingly fueling the city, quenching a thirst for poetry...."

JEAN COCTEAU,
FOREWORD TO
THE NAGEL GUIDE: ITALY.

96-97 Via Condotti as seen from the Spanish Steps of Trinità dei Monti.

TWILIGHT IN ROME: A ROSE-COLORED HAZE

"The rumble of carriage wheels came up from the Piazza di Spagna and the Pincio. A great many people were strolling under the trees in front of the Villa Medici. Two women seated on a stone bench beside the church were keeping watch over some children playing around the obelisk, which shone rosy red under the sunset, and cast a long slanting, blue-gray shadow. The air freshened as the sun sank lower. Farther off, the city stood out golden against the colorless clear sky, which made the cypresses on Monte Mario look jet black."

GABRIELE D'ANNUNZIO,
THE CHILD OF PLEASURE,
LONDON: WILLIAM
HEINEMANN, 1898.

SOLEMN AND MAJESTIC RISES THE GREAT DOME

"I searched with my eyes for a window with a commanding view of the city. I was at the foot of the Pincio. I climbed the grandiose stairway of Trinità dei Monti, recently majestically restored at the wishes of Louis XVIII, and took up residence in the house once occupied by Salvator Rosa, on Via Gregoriana. From the table at which I write I can see three quarters of Rome. Before me, on the other side of the city, the dome of St. Peter's rises regally. In the evening, as it sets I glimpse the sun through the windows of St. Peter's, and half an hour later this wonderful monument is silhouetted against the clearest orange-colored twilight, dominated on high in the sky by the first stars. Nothing on this earth is comparable. The soul is touched and exalts, it is filled with a quiet bliss. I do feel that, to be able to grasp these sensations, one must have loved Rome for a long time. A young man who has never experienced misfortune would not understand them."

STENDHAL,
LES PROMENADES DANS ROME,
PARIS: COLMANN LÉVY
EDITEURS, 1926

101 *The dome of St. Peter's.*

102-103 *The statues of the Dioscuri on the Campidoglio.*

104-105 *An unusual view of Constantine's Arch (fourth century A.D.), with the tower of Palazzo Senatorio (sixteenth century) on the left.*

106-107 *The fountain (eighth century) of Piazza Santa Maria in Trastevere.*

SECRET ROME: AN EMOTION AT EVERY TURN

"In Rome the ruins are not dead. They serve a purpose. They are alive. There is no corner, arch, concealed courtyard, that is not home to some activity."

Jean Cocteau, Foreword to The Nagel Guide: Italy.

108 top Craftsmen in Vicolo dei Cappellari.

108 bottom Craftsmen in Piazza Navona.

108-109 Craftsmen in Piazza Farnese.

A ROMAN IS A ROMAN...

"Rome is popular, but never bourgeois or stupid. Rome seems not to have different social classes. A Roman is a Roman, whether a baker or a Torlonia prince. The Roman aristocracy has nothing to do with that of the rest of the world. Our aristocrats are yokels, they are simpletons. Here all are equal and this makes Rome and the Romans rather unique."

FROM AN INTERVIEW WITH
MONICA VITTI,
ITALIAN ACTRESS.

112 *The market in Campo de' Fiori.*

112-113 *The market in Piazza della Moretta.*

114-115 *The Spanish Steps of Trinità dei Monti (1724-1726).*

116 left A barbershop in Via dei Portoghesi.

116 right An unusual shutter in Via Nazionale.

*116-117 Detail of a doorway
in Via delle Tre Cannelle.*

118 left A window overlooking Via Margutta.

118 right The garden of the Galleria Novella Parigini in Via Margutta.

119 The Osteria Margutta in Via Margutta.

120 left The Fontana della Botte near the Basilica of Santa Maria in Trastevere.

120 top right A fountain at La Sapienza University, in Via degli Staderari.

120 bottom right The fountain in Piazza della Cancelleria.

120-121 The fountain in Via delle Tre Cannelle.

AUSTERE AND NOBLE
AS VIA GIULIA

"I often drank in the beauty of Rome, its monuments, its countryside, certain taverns. I used to live at 149 Via Monserrato. Two steps away was the austere and noble Via Giulia, Piazza Farnese with its extraordinary Palazzo, and the long pathetic Tiber. I regret not having painted more often in the open air and not having done more views of Rome. I did in later years. My paintings of those far-off Roman times were if noting else the honest fruit of a sincere need, of a delicate feeling, and sometimes if I see them again it is with some emotion."

FILIPPO DE PISIS,
"LA PITTURA ROMANA,"
BELTEMPO MAGAZINE.

122-123 *The arch of Palazzo Farnese (sixteenth century) in Via Giulia.*

124-125 *The Campidoglio.*

125 *The dioscuri.*

126-127 Piazza del Quirinale (sixteenth century), the fountain, the obelisk, and the statue of Castor and Pollux.

127 Piazza Navona, detail of a statue on the Fontana dei Fiumi (1650-1651).

RED HOUSES,
BAROQUE MELANCHOLY

"It is the liveliest capital in Europe. You have to drive around it in a carriage, steeped in that torrent of carefree ease that denotes the style of a race which keeps its pace to a stroll even when in a hurry. Apart from the areas I have lived in, the Rome I like most is baroque Rome, especially Piazza Navona. I do like Piazza del Quirinale. Those red houses at dusk, those Roman sunsets that induce melancholy, the colors of Scipione and Mafai, somewhat funereal. This is the special charm of Rome."

FROM AN INTERVIEW WITH
VITTORIO GASSMAN,
ITALIAN ACTOR.

EVERYTHING COMES ALIVE,
ALL IS THROBBING

"Speak to me stones, talk you towering palaces! Roads, utter a word! Genius, do you move no more? Yes, all is within your sacred walls, eternal Rome, alive; only for me is all mysteriously so. Who shall love me, at which window will I see the gracious creature to me passion and solace? Still no indication of the streets along which continuously to and fro to see her I shall sacrifice precious time? Now I observe churches, palaces, ruins, and columns, as a discerning man who from his journey draws active profit. Yet soon it will end, since one temple alone, the temple of love, shall be the one to welcome the initiate. A world you are in truth, Rome; and yet without love the world would not be the world, nor Rome, Rome."

JOHAN WOLFGANG GOETHE,
"ELEGIE ROMANE".

128 The Fontana delle Tartarughe, or Turtle Fountain, (1581-1588), Piazza Mattei.

128-129 Fontana del Tritone, or Fountain of the Triton, (1642), Piazza Barberini.

HIDDEN ROME

"At the corner of the solitary lane, where no sound is heard but the gurgle of an invisible fountain, a lamp dimly illuminates a small Madonna, the odd silver heart shining out from the bunches of withered flowers all around her."

CESARE PASCARELLA
"LE CAMPANE DI RIPETTA,"
PROSE 1880-1890,
TURIN: S.T.E.N., 1920.

130 left A frieze on a house opposite Trevi Fountain.

130 right A glimpse of the German Cemetery, Vatican City.

131 Frieze with the Virgin Mary, Palazzo Chigi (seventeenth century).

THE ETERNAL ROMAN SPIRIT

"The number of masterpieces found in Rome is frightening and overwhelming. One feels even smaller than in the desert."

GUSTAVE FLAUBERT
CORRESPONDENCE DEUXIEME
SÉRIE (1850-1854),
PARIS : BIBLIOTHEQUE
CHARPENTIER, 1907.

132 *Inside the church of Santa Maria in Aracoeli (eighth-fourteenth centuries), Campidoglio.*

133 *Inside the church of San Giovanni in Laterano (fourteenth century).*

134-135 *Detail of Bernini's colonnade in St. Peter's (1656-1667).*

136-137 *The Fontana dei Fiumi (1650-1651), Piazza Navona.*

138-139 *Via dei Fori Imperiali (second century B.C.) with the Torre delle Milizia (eighth century) behind it to the left.*

140 *St. Mark the Evangelist, the Venice's patron saint, is symbolized by a winged lion.*

142-143 *The fertile hills of the "Joyful Region" of Treviso pour out rivers of frothy, sparkling Prosecco, one of the most popular Veneto wines.*

144-145 *The impressive scenery of Mounts Sorapis and Antelao constitutes a worthy backdrop to the magnificent Ampezzo Valley.*

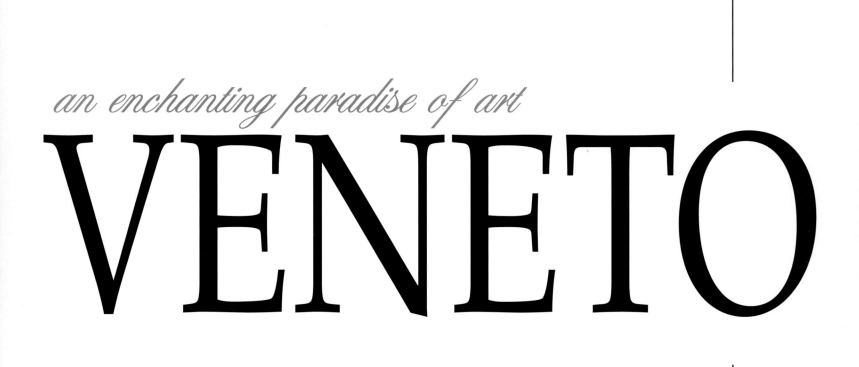

an enchanting paradise of art

VENETO

an enchanting paradise of art

VENETO

CONTENTS

147 The colorful houses on the isle of Burano, famous for lacemaking, welcome visitors and artists looking for peace and an inimitable palette of colors brimming with charm and history.

INTRODUCTION

The many and varied physical characteristics of the Veneto region, which are hard to find on such a large scale in other regions of Italy, make it unique in the true sense of the word. The variety of the landscape embraces mountains, sunny green valleys, rounded shady hills and endless plains, deep rivers and tortuous steams, lakes with a mild climate thanks to the maternal protection of the mountains, and finally the sea, which the Venetians learned to master long ago, making huge profits from trade.

The secret of the immortal charm of this delightful area lies in its diverse contours.
Not only is Veneto rich in tradition and history, but nature has also been generous with its fruits, from the proudly soaring Dolomites
with their permanently snow-capped pinnacles to the delightful Euganean Hills, where
the mud still bears the traces of an ancient volcano, and the hillsides slope gently down

to the shores of Lake Garda, covered with flourishing vineyards. The generosity of Mother Nature has been matched by the skills of people and artists capable of interacting with the surrounding environment without dominating it.

A good example is provided by the buildings designed by Andrea Palladio, one of the many great men born in Veneto. His creations are able to bestow the same artistic dignity on the hills and countryside that buildings of other brilliant men have bestowed on cities. Palladio paid his homage to Veneto outside its towns and cities brimming with art and culture, demonstrating that the craft of the artist cannot detract from the beauty of nature, but only enhance its wonder. Palladio set a trend. His creations have been envied and imitated all over the world. However, as Dante put it, often "matter is deaf to the artist's entreaties" and the raw material which Palladio's imitators lacked ensured the unique nature of "Happy Veneto."

The rivers Adige, Brenta, Piave, and the River Po with its ramified delta, constitute the lifeblood of the waters that nourish and fertilize Veneto's soil. This link between earth and water is even closer in the Venice lagoon.

Here, man has learned how important it is to maintain a strong, healthy relationship with the environment, however hostile, even deviating rivers to prevent them from silting up. Venice certainly presents a unique case of a town that learned at an early stage to fight the land and defend itself against the devastating force of the sea, but that determination, for which it was renowned in the thousand-year-long history of the Venetian Republic, now has to battle against the insensitivity and incompetence of those who have the onerous task of defending the city.

The ancient Venetians saved their land from invasion by barbarians, but have yet to settle who will save Venice from barbarous modernity.

148 top This photo shows an aerial view of Malcesine, a famous resort on the banks of Lake Garda which is visited by many German tourists following in the footsteps of Goethe.

148 bottom Veneto is also a region of magnificent mountain ranges and breathtaking views, as can be seen from this enchanting view of Mount Pelmo, whose impressive peak towers over Val Zoldana.

148-149 A delightful view of Bassano del Grappa with the famous roofed bridge over the River Brenta, designed by Palladio in 1569. The bridge, which has been destroyed and rebuilt countless times, is also famous for sad war songs inspired by the tradition and sacrifices of the Alpine troops.

150-151 The island of St. Giorgio Maggiore, framed by the Gothic arches of the Doge's Palace, is characterized by the harmonious architectural design of Palladio, who masterfully blended art with an exceptionally beautiful natural setting.

151 Everyday life in Verona is symbolized by Piazza delle Erbe, where a colorful throng strolls past before the curious or oblivious gaze of the patrons sitting at the numerous café tables.

152-153 The dazzling splendor of the mosaics in St. Mark's Basilica invites visitors to travel back in their mind's eye to the golden days of old, when Venice acted as a bridge between East and West.

The expression "Happy Veneto" does not mean that Veneto lacks problems. Its good-natured, unsophisticated, hospitable, hard-working inhabitants, to whom Italy owes its current wealth and surprising economic prosperity, as is universally acknowledged, gained that important distinction by virtue of immense, atavistic sacrifices, by the sweat of their brow, and the sad inheritance of the hardships of emigration, which was frequent in the nineteenth century and the early decades of the twentieth.

The region's wealth of tradition, which is still flourishing and proudly cherished, without being in the least contaminated by the ever greater temptations of the tourist market, is explained by the need to alternate hard work with well-deserved convivial recreation. The people of Veneto have fought a constant, hard battle with an environment which,

Cadore assimilated in childhood. Giorgione's Tempest reflects the true poetry of nature, immortalizing the fleeting moment when lightning rends the sky, illuminating a stretch of Veneto countryside to sinister effect. The clear, bright skies of Venice are imprinted on the memory by the precise perspectives of Canaletto's "camera obscura". Perhaps the best example of all is to be found in Turner's Venetian canvases which, with their infinitely intricate allusions, express the unique sensibility common to all great spirits.

The expression "Happy Veneto" is not a cliché, and you don't need to be sitting at a table in the Florian café, looking at one of the loveliest squares in the world, to understand the truth of this existential condition. In fact it's better to be in one of the characteristic inns that abound in the Veneto region, sitting in front of one of the scintillating, perfumed glasses of wine that constitute an invitation to hospitality and socializing. It's here that today's

though magnificent, is sometimes threatening and hostile, always ready to take back the fruits of the labor of generations. It is perhaps this struggle which has left its mark on this population, teaching them the wisdom of calm endurance, even when it means packing their bags and moving to far-reaching places, while still remaining loyal in their hearts to their tormented but no less beloved origins.

"Happy Veneto" also refers to magical, eloquent, bewitching art, delightful in its triumph of color. The region offers an unrivaled, varied range of artistic production, and this miracle manifests in the images, landscapes, and colors imprinted on the hearts and minds of the most sensitive men and then transferred onto canvas, where the whole range of the artist's palette runs riot. Some of Titian's skies are only matched by the colors of the twilight and dawns of

"enlightened travelers" stop on their "Grand Tour" to restore their spirits in the contemplative bliss of a pretty piazza in a Veneto town. There, amid the din of jumbled conversations, where the sound of the region's delightful singsong dialect mingles with that of the bells that toll at regular intervals during the working day, visitors begin to "rub their brains against other people's," to borrow a telling image from Montaigne.

At this point, the photographs can speak for themselves, because the magic eye of the camera not only shoots scenes mechanically, but also, through the sensitivity of the photographer, conveys moments, pathos, and laughter, human landscapes, atmospheres, and subtle enchantments that become memories and patiently wait their turn to be solemnly consecrated as history.

VENICE: SEA, LAGOON, AND HISTORY

154 top The Rialto Bridge, built between 1588 and 1591 according to a design by Antonio Da Ponte, with a single span supporting two rows of shops and three pedestrian lanes, was the only bridge connecting the opposite banks of the Grand Canal until the nineteenth century.

In his *Recitativo Veneziano*, written especially for Fellini's film *Casanova*, poet Andrea Zanzotto paid homage to Venice with a play named after the city, *Regina and Venusia*, and portraying it as born like Aphrodite from the froth of the sea. The erotic nature of this artificial city, brought into the world by the "intelligent hands" of men, who have torn it from its natural element and built it on an unstable, fluid, living element like water, is almost palpable. The little islands of the Venetian archipelago are linked by thousands of support piles made of elm, larch, and oak from the woods of Montello, Cansiglio and Asolano, and the forests of Dalmatia.
This vital reserve of wood and trees, palpitating with life, has been used to construct the body of the city, but it is also the main reason for its incredible fragility, as Venice learned the hard way when a devastating fire recently destroyed the opera house, La Fenice Theater.

Venice is a beautiful city, but like all beautiful things it is fragile. It has a glassy, crystalline nature. Everything there is anomalous, from the shapes of its roads and canals to its curious layout, and something about this quality suggests ancestral love, the primordial origin, the fluidity of the maternal womb, and repressed Oedipus complexes.
Its name and its epithets, including La Serenissima and La Dominante, all allude to a feminine nature. Venice is a city where physical contact is unavoidable. People literally bump into one another in its narrow alleyways, on the bridges crossing the canals, on the lanes along the canals, and in the conspiratorial darkness of a portico, which is perhaps why Casanova decided to be born there.

Many love affairs have been born and died in Venice. Alfred de Musset and George Sand, Lord Byron and his endless procession of concubines, Eleonora Duse and Gabriele D'Annunzio, and many other famous couples have met up here. Over the centuries, Venice has won the reputation of being the only city in the world conducive to love in public places, but it is also the place where passion, after blossoming, soon dies a tragic death.

Even the names of various places bear out this theory, and many of them are ambiguous.

154 center Punta della Dogana, just a stone's throw from the Baroque Chiesa della Madonna della Salute, stretches out into St. Mark's Basin, separating the Grand Canal from the Giudecca Canal.

154 bottom Giudecca Island, seen here in an aerial view, has a narrow, elongated shape, which is why it used to be called "Spinalonga" (long spine). It was once covered with vegetable gardens and vineyards, but became an industrial zone in the late nineteenth century.

154-155 A magnificent view of the quay, the Piazzetta and St. Mark's Square, with the Doge's Palace, the Basilica, and the belltower, affectionately dubbed "the landlord" by Venetians, silhouetted against the sky.

155 bottom From above, Venice looks like a gigantic fish floating on the calm waters of the lagoon. It is a veritable archipelago of islands joined by bridges and manmade surfaces, sometimes supported by a dense network of supporting piles.

156 top Statues and pigeons are predominate in the loveliest view over St. Mark's Basin, a large stretch of water, land, roofs, and sandbanks.

156 bottom The unusual nature of the colors used by artists in the Venetian Republic can only be understood by observing the gradual metamorphosis of the colors on the buildings, as demonstrated by the red brickwork of the bell tower.

156-157 Lonely gondolas moored on the quay, wait to take on hordes of tourists. These unique boats, which inspired the melodious song known as the barcarola, have acted as discreet witnesses to countless passionate love affairs.

157 top right Palazzo Contarini del Bòvolo is named after its unusual outer spiral staircase, reminiscent of a snail (bòvolo in the Venetian dialect).

157 bottom This view of the mouth of the Grand Canal shows the Baroque Chiesa della Salute in a typical winter atmosphere, with a still, leaden, overcast sky and the sun peeping out timidly from behind the clouds.

Ponte delle Tette (Tit Bridge) suggests a lucrative business involving prostitution, which was one of the main pastimes and attractions of Renaissance Venice. There was even a catalogue, intended for the use of strangers, containing a list of the names of the "honored courtesans" and the services they offered. In another secluded spot not far away stands Ponte della Donna Onesta (Honest Woman Bridge), evidently such an unusual condition that it deserved special mention and a street sign all to itself, recorded for eternity on one of the characteristic plates known as ninzioleti (little sheets).

The prodigious sense of getting lost in this labyrinthine structure accentuates the aura of mystery that hovers over Venice, the bewitching old madam, who still wields her irresistible weapons of seduction far and wide. She is bowed down with age and history.
Her wrinkles certainly show, in the cracks in the crumbling brickwork on the canal banks and in the salt deposits encrusted on the façades of

The effect only lasts for a few minutes, but leaves the spectator amazed and enchanted, while the veil of evening falls inexorably like a slow curtain to conclude a spectacular performance.
The only thing missing is the applause, but the sensation remains: by now Venice has won you over, and left its mark on you for all time.

In this real and virtual maze, where the dimension of time does not exist, but disintegrates as in a dream, love is not the only thing that's ephemeral. Everything moves more slowly here.

The steamboats zigzag up and down the Grand Canal at a snail's pace without ever watching the clock, for time has stood still here in Venice. We have just left behind us the ugly, squat railway station, which clashes so unpleasantly with the monumental exuberance of the Baroque façade of the Scalzi church designed by Longhena. As soon as we look right or left, the enchantment begins. There's the eighteenth-century Palazzo Labia, with its blocks of Istria stone dazzling in the sunlight, and on the other side a glimpse of the Orient, where a cavalier nineteenth-century restoration has given an artificial charm to

the buildings, rising steeply upwards as if the water wanted to take back what man had snatched away from it centuries ago. In this interminable contest, the sea bides its time, waiting to get even. It's a perpetual game between Eros and Thanatos, Love and Death, a game repeated daily that enhances the voluptuous melancholy of Venice.

You have to see a sunset in autumn, when the red sun, like a ball of fire, drowns in the calm waters of the lagoon, to understand the beauty of this city and the dualism on which it feeds and lives. From Punta della Dogana the sky turns to flame, the great dome of Chiesa della Salute is silhouetted darkly against the sky, and the clouds form creatures, monsters, and anamorphoses that are reflected in the water and reassembled into spectral shapes like apparitions, almost ghosts, as the fire spreads like a river of lava flowing suddenly out of the crater of a volcano and sweeping away all before it. The red brick of the houses in the Giudecca district turns to a deeper shade charged with color and highlights.

the Turkish Warehouse. This building, on the main road of the city, demonstrates the hospitality of Venice, which allowed its most terrible enemy to set up shop, make a home, and trade freely on Venetian soil. As we approach the Renaissance Palazzo Vendramin Calergi another page of history turns, and the harmonious notes of Richard Wagner echo in the air.

Here, the great composer tragically ended his days before joining the legendary heroes of Valhalla immortalized in his music. Gothic arches embroider the façade of the noblest of the Venetian mansions, which the locals called Ca' d'Oro (House of Gold) as a perpetual sign of admiration. It has now been permanently restored to its original beauty following very careful renovation. At a loop of the canal we come to the crowded, noisy Neo-gothic Fish Market. Then you spot the most famous bridge in Venice, the Rialto, the pulsating heart of frenetic business activity in the past and tourism in the present day, with the rows of shops and colorful stalls of

its markets, which are still surprisingly active in a city that is sadly losing large numbers of residents.

Across the bridge, the magic continues. Each palazzo bears the name of a famous family, which has given Doges to Venice: Dandolo, Loredan, and Grimani. The University now stands in the place where the famous Francesco Foscari once lived, and Carlo Rezzonico, who became Pope with the name of Clement XIII, lived in the Baroque Ca' Rezzonico, where one of the most magnificent museums displaying eighteenth-century works is housed. Every palazzo is a museum, and some have been converted into great exhibition centers, like Palazzo Grassi, whose collection has nothing to fear from comparison with other museums housing art of distant civilizations like those of the Phoenicians, the Celts, and the Greeks, or an immortal master of modern art like Pablo Picasso.

The Gallerie dell'Accademia, which houses the best of Venetian art, with canvases by Titian, Giorgione, Veronese, Tintoretto, Guardi, and Canaletto, is a feast for the eye. From the top of the wooden bridge of the Accademia, inevitably fated to be temporary, we look down on the other symbol of the slow pace of life in Venice, the gondola. Severe in appearance, with that dark color that evokes macabre fantasies, sinuous in its asymmetrical complexity, and designed to be balanced and steered by a single oarsman, it slowly cleaves the water, as if afraid to disturb its calm. It is the Queen of boats, built in accordance with ancient rules and proportions jealously handed down from father to son and concealed in the squeri (boatyards), where the last master carpenters still carve the wood, meticulously following the ancient technique. The gondola remains untouched by the contagion of modernity, and in addition to its use for mere tourism, it continues to demonstrate its eternal practicality in the routes connecting the opposite banks of the Grand Canal.

Even the gondolier's movements follow a strict ritual: the oar is gently submerged with a regular

158-159 Crossing the Grand Canal is like going back through centuries of history. The names of Doges and centuries of art are inextricably linked. For example, the Renaissance Palazzo Dolfin Manin stands close to the late Gothic Palazzo Bembo.

158 bottom left Ca' d'Oro is the most outstanding gem of Venetian Gothic architecture. It is named after the multicolored decorations on the marble, once covered with gilding. The building was last restored in 1984.

158 bottom right, Giorgio Massari, the spiritual heir of Baldassare Longhena, built Palazzo Grassi between 1749 and 1766. This classical, elegant, but cold façade is a precursor to Neoclassicism.

159 top The large ballroom of the Rezzonico family's mansion, demonstrates the megalomania of these eighteenth-century noblemen.

159 bottom The narrow, dark canals that flow into the Grand Canal give access to the luminous marvels of the Venetian palazzi.

splashing sound, dividing the water which immediately closes behind it. This is the magic of Venice.

Venetians born and bred have been taught an important lesson: hurrying is forbidden in this city. Perhaps that's why those who were born in this paradise can never get used to the frenetic pace imposed by the mainland and the big cities.

They can't wait to get home again. Here, loneliness is non-existent; all you have to do is go into the streets, and the crowd immediately swallows you up. Perhaps it's this excessive physical contact that is sometimes disturbing, or perhaps it is the uncivilized use of the city by the inappropriate "hit and run" type of tourism imposed by modern travel agencies, but in Venice it is sufficient to know your way round the streets, with Ariadne's thread as your guide. After a few paces Venetian finds themselves with people who speak their own gentle tongue. You can smell the fragrance of the gargantuan meals prepared in homes and inns off the beaten track, where for once the patrons don't speak German, English, or French but only pure Venetian dialect, even among animals, such as stray cats, dogs, and pigeons. The old "cat lady" calls every puss by name, and each cat answers, slyly meowing and rubbing itself slowly against the old lady's hobbling legs to demonstrate its infinite gratitude. Venice is a city that loves animals. The lagoon also offers shelter to flocks of gleaming black cormorants together with the reluctant little egrets with their aristocratic reserve that perch suspiciously on the sandbanks, and there are seagulls everywhere.

They swoop down into the streets and mingle with the feeding pigeons and some of them even venture timidly into the shops to beg with their impertinent screeching cry. It sometimes makes you wonder whether they don't enjoy the best view of the city.

161 bottom Procession in St. Mark's Square by Gentile Bellini, which belongs to the Miracle of the Cross cycle, portrays a solemn moment in Venetian popular worship.

162 bottom left Palazzo
Pisani-Moretta owes its
charm to the Late Gothic
architecture, enhanced by the
magnificent central double
six-lighted window with its
entwining quatrefoil arches.

162-163 Venice's palazzi
contain art treasures,
exquisite stucco work, and
elegant furnishings, as can be
seen in the delightful
drawing room of Palazzo
Contarini-Fasan,
traditionally known as
"Desdemona's House."
This palazzo is perhaps one
of the smallest of those lining
the Grand Canal, but it is
easily distinguished by its
single-lighted and three-
lighted mullioned windows,
accompanied by little
balconies with a lacy
openwork pattern.

If you climb the bell tower of St. Mark's ("the
landlord" as the Venetians familiarly call it) on a
clear day, you can look out over that stretch of
water, roofs, houses, and steeples and imagine you're
in perpetual flight like those seagulls, the true
dominators of the huge placid lagoon studded with
sandbanks and islands.

How delightful it must be to fly over lanes and
squares, and perch on the pinnacle of a bell tower.
Bell towers abound in Venice, as do churches. Some
are small and austere and others huge, like those
containing the mortal remains of the Doges, such as
the Gothic Church of Saints John and Paul, run by
Dominican monks, or the almost twin church of
Santa Maria Gloriosa dei Frari, named after the
Franciscan Friars Minor. This monumental complex
contains five centuries of Italian history, to which
the divine brush of Titian added the marvelous
Assunta altarpiece. Now, it is time to fly off again
towards St. Mark's Square. There is often too much
of a crowd queuing in front of the Basilica, and too
many groups of Japanese tourists staring upwards,
camera or camcorder at the ready, waiting to capture
the Moors that have punctually sounded the hours
on the Clock Tower with their slow, precise
movements for nearly 500 years.

The eyes are dazzled by the mosaics, from which
light reflects onto the glass of a window of the
Procuratie above the iron tables of the Florian,
Lavena, and Quadri cafés, while the melodies played
by their orchestras linger in the air, often mingled
with the slow, deafening peal of the bells trying to
regain their lost musical supremacy over the Square
that once belonged to them alone.

The Doge's Palace awakens, but except in
occasional historical pageants, we no longer hear the
sound of trumpets and the roll of drums announcing
the Doge's appearance at the window of his majestic
palace, the seat of government, the law courts, and
the Doge's residence, with Gothic arches that appear
to have been designed by a skilled lace maker.

The impressiveness of the building is evident as
soon as the visitor passes through the Gothic Map

162 bottom right Palazzo
Contarini dalle Figure is
named after the two figures
of monsters crushed under
the main balcony. However,
it is interesting not so much
for its Istria stone façade as
for the novelty constituted by
the insertion of a four-lighted
window surmounted by a
tympanum.

163 The Labia family, which
came from Catalonia, made
its fortune in trade. They
spared no expense to fresco
the rooms of their residence
in Campo San Geremia,
commissioning the work
from the expert hand of
Giambattista Tiepolo.

164 top The calm waters of St. Mark's Basin seem to mingle with the sky as the light changes, taking on the same shades and hues, and enhancing the contrast with the monumental buildings reflected in it.
This photo shows Punta della Dogana.

164 center Hippolyte Taine, who visited Venice in 1864, was dazzled by the colors of the lagoon. He wrote that when evening falls, the churches and palazzi grow huge and float on the water like ghosts. This view of the island of St. Giorgio seems to confirm his impression.

164 bottom Motor boats and launches of all kinds add to the swell on the Grand Canal, causing serious damage to the gondolas and even to the foundations of the buildings.

Gate, when its grandiose size is demonstrated and the pattern of the loggias is interrupted by the Giants' Staircase, designed by Antonio Rizzo in the late fifteenth century, with the two statues of Neptune and Mars which are clear allegories for Venetian dominion over land and sea.

Not far away stands the Golden Staircase by Sansovino, which abounds in cherubs and figures of women and symbolizes the magnificence of the Venetian Republic, stuccoes by Alessandro Vittoria literally drowning in gold, the Doge's Apartments and the astonishing atmosphere of the High Council Room, where the huge Paradise canvas, painted by Jacopo Tintoretto with the aid of his son Domenico and Palma the Younger, stands out on the back wall. Visitors entering the Room of the Three State Inquisitors are liable to shudder, and it does not require much imagination to do so, because a small staircase leads to the terrifying Torture Chamber where a sinister rope immediately evokes the agony that was in store for the unfortunate people who fell into disgrace.

The Bridge of Sighs, which crosses the Rio di Palazzo, fires the imagination of incurable romantics, who remember tragic stories of prisoners awaiting trial being taken to the Prisons in the fear of being left to rot forever, condemned to the terrifying damp of the pozzi (well prisons) or forced to dream of adventurous escapes from the piombi (lead prisons) if they were to avoid certain death.

At the foot of Ponte della Paglia (Straw Bridge) lies the wide Riva degli Schiavoni, which commemorates sailors from Schiavonia (now Dalmatia). This panoramic route running alongside St. Mark's Basin is lined with the most famous hotels in Venetian tradition: the Danieli, the Gabrieli, and the Londra. The long road continues alongside the Parish Church of St. Zaccaria until it makes a triumphant entrance into St. Mark's Square. Today, the only inhabitants of this past are tourists, who rush ecstatically from one route to another, dazed by the incredible variety of all this splendor.

164-165 The colorful "column" or "palazzo" posts which can be seen in the foreground, often decorated with friezes and coats-of-arms, are used as mooring posts for gondolas and to mark the boundary of the waters owned by each palazzo.

165 bottom Rio di San Trovaso with Ponte delle Meravegie (Bridge of Marvels). The bridge is actually named after Palazzo Maravegia, owned by the Maravegia family, although some say it takes its name from wondrous events that occurred on that stretch of the canal.

Sometimes they stop and rest in the Piazzetta, between two tall monoliths of Oriental granite that dominate the quay and St. Mark's Basin. On one column stands a winged lion, which in reality is perhaps an ancient Chinese chimera, and on the other stands the statue of St. Todaro (Theodore), a Byzantine saint and the first patron saint of the city. Here, it is easy to imagine that you are inside a painting by Guardi or Canaletto, perhaps during the Easter Thursday Festival, amid tumblers, acrobats, charlatans, and fortune-tellers. We can also meditate on the priceless treasures in the Libreria Sansoviana, designed by Jacopo Sansovino and begun in 1537 to house the precious collections, initially donated by Cardinal Bessarione. Since 1904 the library has been extensively reorganized, and is now partly housed in the neighboring rooms of Sansovino's Mint. St. Mark's National Library, with a million books, 13,000 manuscripts, many of them decorated with exquisite miniatures, and 3,000 incunabula, is a popular place of pilgrimage for book lovers from all over the world. A group of curious souls are usually waiting patiently in front of the Loggetta to climb the bell tower, and there's no better way of passing the time than examining the reliefs, which include an interpretation of Venice in the form of Justice, an obvious allegory of good government.

This was how the sculptor depicted the ideal of the perfect republic, which only Venice believed itself capable of embodying. Another huge queue usually takes root on the paving stones in front of the Basilica. The tourists are sometimes forced to stand on the rickety gangways normally used when the town center had flooded, but that have become permanent fixtures with time, and will no doubt be protected by the Historic Monuments Inspectorate sooner or later.

166

166-167 The Rialto fish market is still the most popular meeting place for Venetians, and the whole area is crammed with stalls offering a choice selection of sea and lagoon fish.

167 bottom The exquisite gondolas are a source of wealth and income for the gondoliers, and therefore receive the kind of treatment normally lavished on custom-built sports cars on the mainland.

168 top left The terrible Venetian prisons were divided into piombi (lead prisons), named after the lead covering the roof tiles, and pozzi (well prisons) like the one seen in the photo, with small, low-ceilinged, unhealthy cells where death came as a happy release.

168 top right From the portico on the piano nobile the magnificent loggia of the Ca' d'Oro resembles a fragile spider's web which, like a lense, filters and fragments the wonderful view over the Grand Canal.

168 center At the Doge's palace, Vittore Carpaccio asserted the rule of the Venetian Republic over land and sea, depicting the symbol of the city's patron saint, the winged lion, with its front paws resting firmly on land, and its hind paws on the sea.

In the meantime, they have the opportunity to learn to distinguish the mosaics, like those on the bowl-shaped vault above the main door of Sant'Alipio, among the oldest on the façade, which include the Procession bearing S. Mark to the Basilica, or to see a replica of the gleaming bronze chariot brought to Venice from Constantinople in 1204, the original of which can be admired later in St. Mark's Museum. Waiting in line will eventually bear fruit. It is definitely worthwhile, because the mosaics in the atrium are breathtaking; the mosaic of the Creation, divided into three concentric circular bands, is particularly impressive, as are the Stories of Noah, the ark, and the great flood.
The interior is a feast for the eye too, with the Pentecost and Ascension Domes and the dazzling Gold Altarpiece. Now, the Stendhal Syndrome begins to take effect.

There are often far too many people in the Square and it would be best to fly off with one of the seagulls to the island of San Giorgio, soaring over the churchyard with its geometrical, perspective paving. Then, from the roof of the classic church designed by Palladio it could swoop right into the heart of La Giudecca, which features another masterpiece by the great architect, the Church of the Redeemer, with its impressive scenic staircase.

168 bottom The Golden Staircase at the Doge's Palace, which was begun in 1554 using a design by Sansovino and later continued by Scarpagnino, was so called because of the abundance of gold and white stucco decoration.

169 The Doge's Palace was the prestigious seat of government in the Venetian Republic, symbolizing its power. The Venetians also turned it into an artistic center, and it was not only the residence of the Doge, but also the headquarters of the Republic's judiciary.

This Church was erected by the Senate as a votive offering to give thanks for the end of the terrible plague of 1576.

Finally, taking flight again, allowing itself to be blown along by the agile currents and winds, the feathered master of the lagoon gazes towards the endless neat rows of vines and vegetable gardens tended by monks, far, far away.

The Lido awaits the flight of the gull with its famous beaches, magnificent Art Nouveau villas and luxury hotels, synonymous with the decadent atmosphere described by Thomas Mann, along with the wild dunes of the Alberonis. Flying back, it can observe Venice from above, as if the city were the biggest fish in the world floating on the sea, with its snaky intestines of placid water instead of bones. This watery outlet, where the workshops of the Arsenal flourished long ago, was once much more attractive, with its sailing ships, armed galleys, and sails unfurled in the wind, back in the days when

the lion of Saint Mark, rampant on the glorious banner, roared and unsheathed its claws. Now, it's milder and has adopted a "crablike" pose, as the locals put it; the lion has lost his claws and learned to feed on resignation.

"What an odd city this is," wrote Jean Cocteau, "where lions fly and pigeons walk!" This marvelous paradox is hard to understand, even for a seagull, so perhaps it's just as well to seek Venice elsewhere, above the high roofs of the very first skyscrapers in history, the Jewish homes in the Ghetto. This magnificent community had its own pawnshops and modest dwellings, together with splendid synagogues built between 1500 and the mid-seventeenth century: the German and Canton Shuls for worship in accordance with the Ashkenazi rite, the Italian Scola in accordance with the Italian rite, and the Levantine and Spanish Shuls in accordance with the Sephardic rite.

Venice holds the unenviable record of having coined the terrible word ghetto, which derives from the fact that foundries (called geti in Venetian dialect) once stood in the circumscribed area assigned to the construction of residential buildings and shops. However, it must be said in its defence that the Venetian Republic was far more tolerant towards the Jewish community than many other countries, as demonstrated by the profusion of art and culture that can still be admired in the Jewish Museum.

A short distance away in the Cannaregio district lies Campo dei Mori, an odd little piazza that transports us into the midst of the Levant.

Here, blood-red brick issues from niches resembling open wounds in the walls of old houses with crumbling plaster, and characters dressed in oriental costumes and wearing turbans look down on us. They're merchants, who look like something out of a play by Goldoni.

Can it be the Impresario of Smyrna, or the Armenian Abagiggi from Women's Gossip, with his incomprehensible Armenian dialect?

170 This portrait of Doge Foscari kneeling before the lion, a copy of a work by Luigi Ferrari painted in 1885, is situated above the Map Gate, the majestic entrance to the Doge's Palace designed by Bartolomeo Bon. The Gate is so called because it stands near the State Map Department's depots and archives.

171 left This Late Roman porphyry group of the Tetrarchs or Moors on the surviving corner tower of the Doge's Palace is traditionally said to portray Diocletian and the other three Emperors who reigned with him.

171 top right Justice is solemnly portrayed in a Gothic bas-relief in the Doge's Palace, situated in the quatrefoil of the loggia

and attributed to Michelino da Besozzo or the Bon School.

171 center right Four Archangels are portrayed in the corner sculptures of the Doge's Palace. This photo shows the Archangel Michael above the scene of the Original Sin. The capitals and corner reliefs were intended by the clients to have a mainly educational function.

171 bottom right L'Ebrezza di Noè (The Drunkenness of Noah an allegory of indulgence), a sculpture by Lombard masters of the fourteenth/fifteenth century, stands on the corner of the Doge's Palace nearest Ponte della Paglia (Straw Bridge), with the Bridge of Sighs in the background.

Historians had great difficulty in deciphering the puzzle, and eventually agreed that the figures portray three brothers from the Mastelli family, traders from Peloponnesus who owned a palace nearby. Its bas-relief portraying an oriental merchant with a camel still surprises those who venture into these remote parts of the city.

Venice was the gateway to the East. Its merchants traveled everywhere, and in every Venetian there is a drop of the blood of these travelers of old, the best known of whom is Marco Polo. If anyone still alleges that the tales told in Polo's book Million are merely fantasies or tall stories, he should visit these places and consider the remnants of the communities scattered all over Venice, such as the Greek, Turkish, and Armenian communities which had warehouses, churche, and even islands of their own in this cosmopolitan city. Why were all these people so happy in Venice that they made it their home? Undoubtedly because in Venice they could breathe a Levantine air, an oriental magic produced by centuries of coexistence and trade, which introduced half Europe to products once rare or wholly unknown, such as purple, exquisite fabrics, hides, and above all, costly spices.

To go even further back in time, while much of Europe was united in a rigid feudal structure under Charlemagne and civilization had escaped from the Dark Ages by the skin of its teeth, these strips of islands, the mainland and the stinking, unhealthy, inhospitable marshes which formed the nascent Venice recognized Byzantium as the only true heir of ancient civilization, which was how the city came to act as a bridge between East and West.

172 top The exquisite coffered ceiling of the Senate Hall in the Doge's Palace was finely carved and decorated profusely with gold to demonstrate the power and wealth of the Venetian Republic to visitors.

172 bottom The wealth of decoration on the vault and the stuccoes depicting Victory in the Sala dell'Anticollegio enabled guests to while away the time before being received by the Doge.

172-173 The Venetian nobility, who ruled the Republic, met in the impressive High Council Room of the Doge's Palace where they sat on benches arranged lengthwise. The assembly, chaired by the Doge and the Lords, passed laws and elected the most important State officials.

173 bottom left The Lords used to receive foreign ambassadors, and Venetian ambassadors returning from their posts, in the College Room, built by Antonio Da Ponte according to a design by Palladio and decorated with canvases by Paolo Veronese on the ceiling.

173 bottom right Another prestigious antechamber in the Doge's Palace was the Hall of Four Doors, so called because of its four monumental doors. However, its greatest attraction were the frescoes on the ceiling, painted by Tintoretto according to a design by Sansovino.

To confirm their loyalty, the Venetians used geometrical tesserae of colored marble, obtained from the Byzantine provinces by robbery, piracy, or honest trade, to form mosaics on the floors of its Basilica and churches. More mosaics glittering with gold, plus enamels, Byzantine icons, precious reliquaries, perfume burners, processional lamps of fine Oriental craftsmanship, and miniatures poured into the coffers of the state and enriched the treasury of Saint Mark. That is why the Orient is ever so present in Venice.

Coming back to reality after this historical digression, prompted by the lure of a magical corner of Venice far away, composure can be regained in the monastic solitude of the Madonna dell'Orto, and admire the pretty Gothic façade in which the warm shades of the pink brickwork enhance the white marble decorations of this church, filled with works by Jacopo Robusti, known as Tintoretto, who lived in Campo dei Mori and rests in peace here. Fortunately, the noisy, intrusive tourists have not yet discovered this address.

But while ordinary mortals in search of prodigies are resigned to picking their way along an endless gangway crossing the water right in the middle of the lagoon, fancifully believing that they can continue their trip as far as "glassy Murano," the seagull will leave to continue his daily patrol of the city as far as the colored houses of Burano, off towards Torcello, far, far away towards the origins of history.

174-175 St. Mark's Basilica, amazingly reminiscent of the East and Byzantium, is the symbol of this city, the Doge's chapel of the palatium, a place of worship, but above all a treasure trove of the arts. The majestic building, inspired by the Twelve Apostles in Constantinople, with its five domes, was consecrated in 1094, while Vitale Falier was Doge.

174 bottom left From the top of the Basilica one of the horses in the copy of the famous four-horse bronze chariot brought to Venice from Constantinople seems about to take wing over the piazza, which is crowded with tourists basking in the early morning sun at the tables of the famous cafés.

174 bottom right The winged lions, walking, rampant, or "crablike," which are representations of St. Mark the Evangelist, are found everywhere in the places consecrated to his legend.

175 top From the top of the clock tower, the Moors have punctually struck the hours for almost 500 years. The tower, which

was built by demolishing two arches of the Procuratie Vecchie, dates from 1499.

175 bottom The sun reflects off the mosaics of the Basilica, producing dazzling, iridescent highlights, demonstrating what Lord Byron meant when he wrote that in order to penetrate the secrets of Venice, you have to look to the Levant.

176 top *The mosaics of St. Mark's cover some 86,000 square feet of the building, so that visitors can walk among the symbols of the Christian faith.*

176 center *The bronze four-horse chariot which was brought to Venice from Constantinople in 1204 has been lovingly restored, and is now on display in St. Mark's Museum.*

176 bottom *Although the exquisite mosaic decoration appears to be fragmented into a number of different legends, according to experts it actually recounts a single tale inspired by the prophetic doctrines of theologian monk Gioacchino da Fiore.*

176-177 *The impressive Gothic iconostasis of Pierpaolo and Iacobello Dalle Masegne, with 14 statues (the 12 Apostles, the Virgin Mary, and St. Mark) on either side of the Crucifix, stands in the nave of the Basilica.*

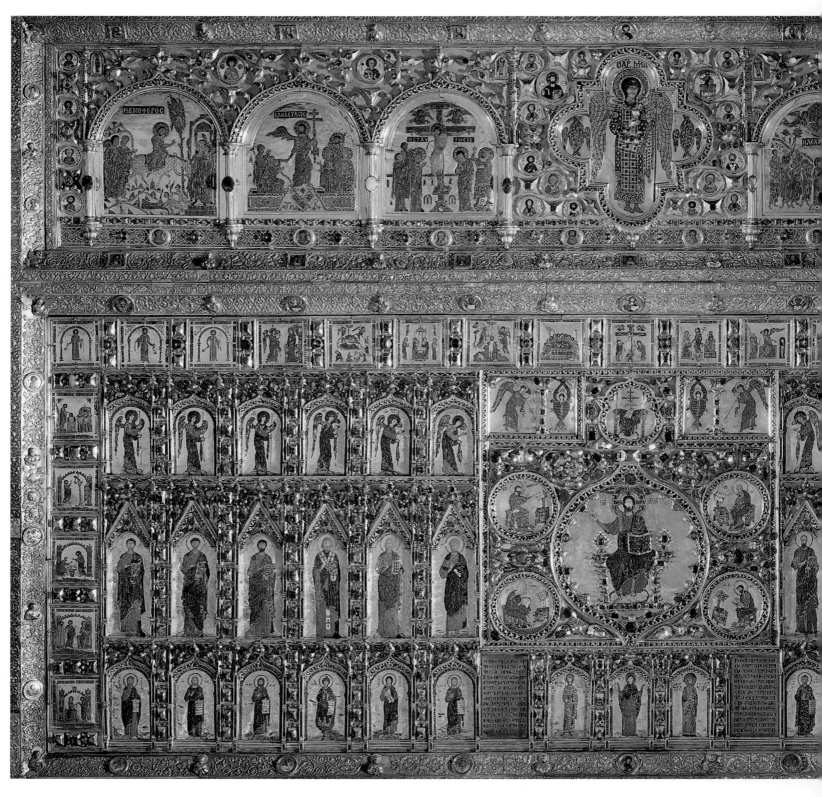

178-179 *The Pala d'Oro stands in all its glory behind the high altar of the Basilica. This gold altarpiece is a masterpiece of Byzantine and Venetian gold-work, to which goldsmith Giovanni Paolo Boninsegna added a gilded silver Gothic structure studded with rare pearls, precious stones, and enamel.*

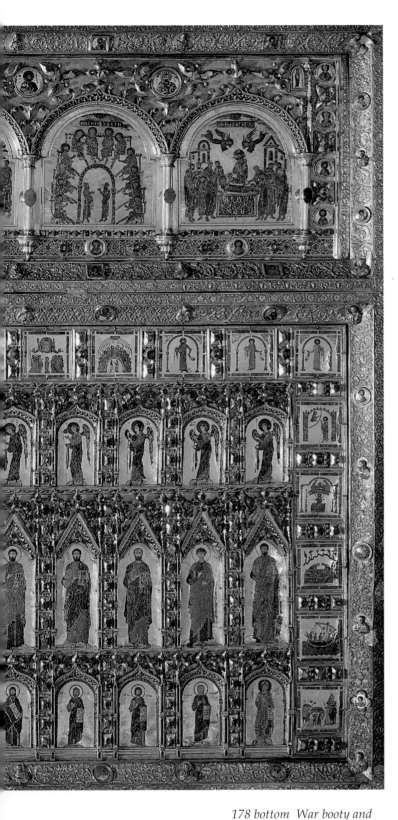

179 top The priceless silver and gilded enamel icon of the Archangel Michael, a masterpiece by eleventh-century Byzantine goldsmiths, is one of the most exquisite pieces displayed in the Treasury of St. Mark's.

179 bottom The half-length portrait of the Archangel Michael portrayed in this icon from Constantinople is another of the exquisite Byzantine gold works from the first half of the eleventh century which have always been present in St. Mark's Treasury.

178 bottom War booty and gifts flooded into Venice together with exquisite marble, especially following the sack of Constantinople. In this way, liturgical articles and reliquaries accumulated over the centuries to form one of the greatest treasures in Christendom.

180-181 Caffé Florian, with its interiors, pretty rooms, nineteenth-century décor, and fancy decorations, including famous personalities and fanciful Oriental figures, gives a wonderful view of one of the most beautiful squares in the world.

180 bottom In winter Venice is shrouded in darkness at an early hour. All that remains to light the city are the characteristic street lamps with their pale light that produces a magical atmosphere, and sometimes throws sinister shadows onto the monumental buildings.

181 top The Lavena café under the Procuratie Vecchie is known as the "musicians' café." It owes much of its fame to a famous customer, Richard Wagner, who took a table in the upper loggia every day.

181 bottom On December 29, 1720, an unknown coffeehouse proprietor called Floriano Francesconi opened his café under the Procuratie Nuove, unaware that he was creating an institution.

182 top The sky is dark and threatening, the water an olive color, the roofs covered with a sprinkling of snow, and an icy north wind is blowing, but a sudden break in the clouds allows the sun to shine through, enhancing the attractive church of St. Maria della Salute.

182 center Dazzling white snow is in unusual contrast with the black gondolas moored, bereft of tourists, in Bacino Orseolo.

182 bottom A gondola in the snow seems to be masked, and it's no accident that it takes on the same sinister colors as the eighteenth-century Venetian "cloak and domino" costume.

182-183 Snow rarely falls in Venice, but when it does, it attracts nationwide interest. It changes the face of the city, as seen in this attractive picture that portrays Saint George Church against the background of the columns of Mark and Todaro.

183 bottom left St. Mark's Square, covered with a fine layer of snow, attracts a crowd of onlookers who breathe the strange odor of the biting cold and look at the glistening domes of the Basilica. Only the Moors, at the top of the Clock Tower, appear to be disturbed in their centuries-old task by the color white, to which they are unaccustomed.

183 bottom right The statue of Niccolò Tommaseo, one of the heroes of the 1848 revolution, looks down with an austere gaze onto the huge, empty Campo di Santo Stefano on a winter's day.

184-185 This picture of the jetty with empty gondolas evokes ancient memories, such as that of Giacomo Casanova being but a stone's throw from the Doge's Palace, ready to repeat his escape from the cells of the piombi for eternity.

186 top St. Mark's Square buzzes with life at night. The melodramatic notes of La Traviata linger on the air at the Florian café, while a frenzied can-can is played at the Quadri, and the Moors wait to say goodnight to this deafening but melodious cacophany.

186 bottom Ca' Dario, one of the palazzi lining the Grand Canal, stands out not only for its multicolored Renaissance marble, but also for the romantically sinister curse said to afflict its owners, who have died violent deaths.

186-187 The blend of music played by three café orchestras turns St. Mark's Square into the loveliest ballroom in the world, where a huge virtual dome encloses the sound of music together with a babble of voices speaking every known language.

187 bottom Warm nocturnal shades are reflected in the trachyte paving slabs of the harbor, while a cold greenish light unnaturally illuminates the Palladian façade of the Church of St. Giorgio Maggiore.

ISLANDS, BEACHES, THE LAGOON, AND THE DELTA

The charm of the lagoon is partly due to the incredible variability of its physical surroundings. Its colors change from one moment to the next, its clarity and its waters rise and fall according to the tides, driven by the warm sirocco winds to lap and invade the trachyte slabs that pave the streets and the Istrian stone that forms the canal banks, leaving nothing untouched, even disturbing the religious peace of the Basilica and its patron saint. The crystal-clear air after a summer cloudburst reminds us that the mountains of Veneto are not that far away, and looking towards the horizon from the Lido or the Fondamenta Nuove, sharp undulating peaks can be discerned. Taking up the oars of a boat and rowing out to Murano or even further, beyond the sandbanks, there are abandoned islands, which have housed lazarettos and important hermitages over the centuries. The mountains seem to have taken refuge on Torcello, and upon reaching that archaically beautiful island, perhaps it will be possible to reach out as if to touch one of the many mirages that Venice so subtly distributes.

188-189 In this delightful aerial view, Burano Island and its labyrinth of bridges and canals looks like a miniature Venice, with its numerous campielli (little squares) and a single piazza named after its most famous citizen, Baldassarre Galuppi.

188 bottom Burano is a riot of color, and its simple fishermen have inherited the magical gift of borrowing the iridescent shades of the lagoon to paint the façades of their homes in strong hues.

189 There is an artistic atmosphere in the air at Burano, which is indeed an artists' colony. The artists who have lived there include Pio Semeghini, Filippo De Pisi, and Gino Rossi, who lived in the famous inn of Romano Barbaro.

190-191 and 190 bottom
The riot of color on Burano is!and is manifested in numerous ways, from the gaudy hues of the boats to the amazing creativity with which characters and names are drawn on their hulls.

191 top Fishing nets and trammels, left to dry in the sun or hung out in a meadow with the washing, are a common sight on Burano island.

191 center In this remote corner of the lagoon, the changing highlights and rays of sunset inspire the imagination with the beauty of nature.

191 bottom In this paradise of art, even a humble bas-relief, considered almost as a family coat-of-arms by a Burano resident, acquires tone and strength, enhanced by the intense color contrast.

The imagination runs riot in this city. It is so hard to explain that even a second book would not suffice. The secret is not to run aground on the sandbanks of rationality.

A short stretch of the lagoon separates Venice from Murano, the island where "Venetian glass" is made and that is one of the most popular destinations for tourists on package tours to Venice. Its busy furnaces continually churn out all kinds of articles, from ornaments to lamps, from fragile glasses to heavy sculptures, often inspired by famous painters and designers. But Murano also offers art, great art. It's a miniature Venice, with its very own meandering Grand Canal overlooked by houses, factories, and a few palazzi which, apart from the ravages of time, still display the glories of their magnificent past, and also convey the impression that the island's prosperity began at a very early date.

The magnificent church of Saints Mary and Donato, one of the most characteristic examples of Veneto-Byzantine style, was built by the descendants of Murano's founders, refugees from Altino, and later from Oderzo, who fled from the invading Lombard hordes, as a way of paying homage to the land where their ancestors found shelter.

When it leaves the last landing-stage on "red" Murano, the steamboat slowly ploughs through the liquid plain, studded with sandbanks covered in sunscorched vegetation and islands with weeping ruins, the last vestiges of ancient communities now extinct, on its way to vibrant Burano. The island of color, an ancient fishing village, has become an artists' colony precisely because it is so colorful. It is a delightful little island, with narrow streets, arched porticoes, miniature canals, washing and fishing nets strung out in the meadows to dry in the sun, and a melodious dialect which, like the language of love, communicates to the heart.

The island's most famous citizen could only be a great musician like Baldassare Galuppi who, proudly mindful of his birthplace, took the name of Buranello. Torcello is right in front of Burano, and in a few

192-193 Murano, a densely populated island in the lagoon and home of the art of glass-blowing, was founded during the Lombard invasion by a group of refugees from Altino, who called it Amurianum after one of the gates of their city.

192 bottom The Pellestrina littoral, between the ports of Malamocco and Chioggia, with its monumental murazzi (a kind of marble breakwater), demonstrates the Venetians' amazing ability to cope with the threat represented by the sea.

193 top The "pathways" through the lagoon are indicated by the characteristic bricole, sets of wooden poles tied to one another which mark the boundaries of the canals and act as maritime signals.

193 bottom The magnificent external apse of the church of Saints Maria and Donato in Murano, with a portico featuring niches and coupled columns and the bell tower, constitutes one of the best surviving examples of Venetian-Byzantine art, with its blend of Byzantine and Romanesque characteristics and architectural motifs.

minutes it is possible to go ashore to disturb the ancient peace and trample the grassy meadows in which vestiges of an impressive civilization survive.

It is hard to imagine that New Altino, where refugees from the nearby mainland found safety when they fled from the barbarians, could once have had a population of 20,000, as the chronicles report. However, without that impressive community, which had its own bishop and tribune, Torcello would perhaps never have enjoyed the prosperity it needed to sponsor the creation of such marvelous architecture. The delightful little piazza with "Attila's chair" (the seat used by the tribunes when administering the law), the most profaned and photographed sight in Italy, has everything, from the fourteenth-century Council and Archive buildings, which now house an important museum displaying archaeological relics from the Roman, early Christian, and late Medieval periods, to the religious atmosphere of the little church of Santa Fosca and the monumental complex of the Cathedral of Santa Maria Assunta. However, it is the mosaic of the Universal Judgement that really takes the visitor's breath away.

It is easy to understand why a writer like Ernest Hemingway found the peace and quiet he needed to write the best parts of his novel Across The River

And Into The Trees in this very hermitage, immersed in nature, peace, spirituality, and history.

From Burano, a convenient motor launch takes us on a short but enjoyable trip across the still waters of the lagoon to Punta Sabbioni, a seaside resort that stretches as far as Cavallino, once part of Venice but now an independent municipality. It boasts famous glasshouses that grow spring vegetables and above all numerous campsites, assiduously frequented by regular customers, mostly Germans, who transform these shores into a German-speaking colony as far as Lido di Jesolo in the summer months.

Lido di Jesolo is the loveliest beach in the Venice area, and is a main attraction because of its wealth of hotels and modern bathing establishments which offer tourists an endless variety of activities, sports, and entertainment, from riding stables to tennis courts, from swimming pools with dizzyingly steep water slides to famous restaurants and discos for lovers of night life. Beyond the Piave estuary lies the more recently developed resort of Eraclea Mare.

This magnificent sandy coastline with its highly popular bathing establishments also offers some very attractive spots of historical interest like the ancient town of Caorle, whose unusual cylindrical brick bell-tower with its conical spire provides a look-out point over the vast waters of the Adriatic.

The Venice Lido, with its exclusive bathing establishments, was once the most popular beach with the international jet set.

However, its popularity gradually declined in favor of brand-new facilities that met the demands of mass tourism more efficiently. It has now been converted into a huge residential center for Venetians, although the original, attractive Art Nouveau villas and hotels like Grand Hotel Des Bains and the Excelsior Palace Hotel, with its oriental look, still survive.

The island rests on the laurels of its magnificent past, and is now satisfied to be back in the limelight once a year during the International Film Festival. Proceeding to the end of the Lido, a boat can be borded at the picturesque medieval town of Malamocco, named after the ancient Doge's residence of Metamauco, where Charlemagne's son Pippin suffered a crushing defeat when his troops were surrounded by the more agile Venetian vessels. The slaughter was horrific, as testified to by the name of Canal Orfano (Orphan Canal), so called to commemorate the Frankish children orphaned in the battle.

A catastrophe then destroyed Metamauco, which sank into the sea and disappeared forever. It was replaced by the delightful Malamocco, which is proud of its Palazzo Pretorio, containing the mayor's offices, the piazza with the Church of St. Maria Assunta, and the characteristic avenue called Merceria which runs through alleys and piazzas to the pretty Ponte di Borgo.

196 top The Venice Lido beach became one of the favorite resorts with the new breed of vacationers in the early twentieth century when the therapeutic properties of sea bathing were discovered. In just under a decade the island became a showplace for the new Art Nouveau style: villas, houses, and great hotels totally changed its original appearance. This photo shows the oriental-looking Excelsior Hotel, opened in July 1907, which looks like a cross between the excesses of Byzantine architecture and a vaguely Turkish design.

196 center Lido di Jesolo, with its famous beaches, clean, manicured sand, ultra-modern bathing establishments, and wealth of top-level sports facilities, is one of the most prestigious Adriatic resorts.

196 bottom Pellestrina, on the lagoon front, offers this long, densely-packed row of fishermen's cottages, with their façades painted in deep, gaudy colors.

196-197 Fishing boats rest at their moorings in the marina, and on this clear, bright day the unmistakable cylindrical shape of Caorle Cathedral's bell tower stands out clearly against the background.

Heading to the south, Pellestrina, a fisherman's island, is a strip of land with numerous arms jutting out into the sea.

These murazzi, great walls made of marble blocks cemented with pozzolana, were the pride of the ancient Venetians, built ausu romano, aere veneto (in the Roman style with Venetian cash) to defend the lagoon. Another commemorative tablet dated 1751 proudly states in Latin, "The keepers of the waters laid colossal blocks of solid marble against the sea so that the sacred estuaries, the site of the city and of freedom, may be preserved in perpetuity." Tradition has it that after the Chioggia war, four families (the Busetto, Vianello, Zennaro, and Scarpa families) began to rebuild Pellestrina. Everyone on Pellestrina now has one of these surnames, as do the four "quarters" into which the island is divided.

These stubborn but hospitable people have their own dialect, which remains distinct from Venetian and outright disdainful of the Chioggia dialect.

They are tough people, who came face to face with death during the catastrophic storm of 1966, when the sea threatened to submerge the island together with Venice.

Yet, the people of Pellestrina stay. They are attached to their homes and their possessions, like the seaweed that almost clings to their homes, although the island lacks even the most basic, essential amenities and they have to depend on the local markets of the Venice Lido and Chioggia to do their shopping.

The last stop on the island is a small cemetery, too small for all the people so attached to this strip of the lagoon, after which a last promontory narrows towards Caroman, a vernacular corruption of Ca' Romana (Roman House). Sailing between the posts that mark the boundary of the canal and the odd buildings on stilts where fishing equipment is kept, the colors of the water change, and the roofs and spires of Chioggia can be seen in the distance.

Chioggia, the ancient Roman Clodia, is given a majestic appearance by the effects of time and centuriation (the Roman division of land into hundreds). The intersecting Roman roads, the cardo and decumanus, with dozens of little lanes branching off from the bustling Corso del Popolo, transform the layout of the town into a dense herringbone-shaped latticework. This fish metaphor and the inevitable comparison with its aristocratic neighbor suggest that the town is a "little Venice." However, this comparison is not appreciated by its inhabitants, who have no wish to resemble anyone, least of all the Venetians, who in the past granted Chioggia institutions similar to their own but totally devoid of political content, so that its fictitious independence was totally crushed by continual interference from the mayor, who held the central power.

The people of Chioggia have a sanguine nature, a skin dried by long exposure to the sun and the dazzling blue-green water, and talk loudly in a melodious, colorful, sing-song dialect. This habit, acquired over the centuries by a population of fishermen who had to shout from one boat to another and one bank to another, has been retained by the elderly out of inertia and inherited by their descendents. The quarrelsome but good-hearted nature of the people of Chioggia was well understood by a young Venetian who obtained his first job as Assistant Registrar of the Criminal Court, Carlo Goldoni, destined to become a famous playwright.

There's no lack of fish and fishing in Chioggia.

The very air is impregnated with them, and the rich vocabulary of the Chioggia dialect has numerous words for them. Perhaps attracted by the fish, at the quay near Ponte di Vigo a curious lion that bears no resemblance to the emblem of Saint Mark, but looks for all the world like a cat, welcomes visitors.

"The Chioggia moggy" looks slyly at us, waiting there indifferent to criticism and unmoved by insult, gazing at the sky as if trying to divert the marùbio (tempest), the terror of sailors, portrayed in thousands of colorful, naïve votive offerings displayed for popular veneration in the Church of San Domenico.

Thronging the crowded streets, cafés, and inns of Canal Vena, lined with fishing boats, nets, and trammels, baskets firmly imprison struggling crabs which, according to the local dialect, develop from strussi (used as fish bait) to spiantani and then shed their skins to become the delectable moléche. Old men hunched stiffly in the taverns amuse themselves by telling repetitive tales of long-ago feats at sea, while the fumes and fog from their meerschaum pipes shroud them in sadness and resignation.

Their stories of hardship and poverty are hard to understand nowadays, in our comfortable, wealthy society, but their bitterness is soon dispelled over a glass of wine. There, amid the confused hum of conversations, the "sweet sound of life" can be heard placidly flowing by.

Eleonora Duse's grandfather Luigi, the last representative of the noble dynasty of Commedia dell'Arte, lived in one of the lanes running perpendicular to Canal Vena. He acted with an amateur dramatic society, then joined a repertory company and spawned a whole family of actors. Applauded on stage and even mentioned by George Sand in Histoire De Ma Vie, he certainly never expected to be remembered as the august ancestor of one of the greatest actresses of the twentieh century. He could have been born nowhere else but in this theatrical city, where Carlo Goldoni looked out of his window onto Corso del Popolo every day and smiled as he watched the hard-working people of Chioggia with their drawling dialect, who were forced to invent imaginative nicknames for themselves (or "aliases," as they are called locally) because so many of them have the same surnames.

198 top This wide-angle aerial view clearly shows the unusual structure of Chioggia, deriving from its remote Roman origins, which makes it look oddly like a fishbone.

198 bottom Large, calm reaches of sandbanks covered with sparse vegetation make patterns on the blue waters of the lagoon, and provide the ideal habitat for seagulls.

199 Canal Vena is one of the most characteristic spots in Chioggia, with its numerous fishing boats, nets hanging out on the bricole, fruit and vegetable stalls, and perpendicular lanes, always buzzing with life.

Whatever happened to the colorful bragozzi, the characteristic fishing boats? A fleet is now anchored in Canal Lombardo which runs parallel to the main street, its forest of masts bristling with the most sophisticated fishing and navigation technologies.

The poor old bragozzo has become merely a souvenir, a model sold to tourists or a cult object for rich collectors who like to stand out from the crowd and from real fishermen. They sail proudly over the waters of the port like ghosts, flying gaudy flags and colorful red and ochre sails bearing the emblems and coats-of-arms of days gone by. Before leaving Chioggia, it is worth crossing the long bridge with the Island of Union in the middle (an inappropriate name if ever there was one), a long umbilical cord that links Chioggia to Sottomarina, where some equally odd people await.

However, it is important to drop the first part of the name of the town upon crossing that bridge because the people of Sottomarina call themselves marinanti and will be very annoyed if they are called anything else.

Leaving behind the bickering of these populations, condemned to be eternally quarrelsome in accordance with literary tradition, one can travel to Polesine, the southernmost tip of Veneto, where the last reaches of the Po flow across the plain to the sea, and the great river "finds peace with all its followers" as Dante put it (Inferno, V 98).

The plain lying between the Rivers Adige and Po is composed of vast wetlands formed over geological time by the accumulation of silt deposited by the two great rivers. Although this abundance of water is vital for agricultural purposes, it is also a cause of concern.

The administrators of the past decided that these waters should be regulated with embankments and artificial canals to avoid disaster, which is why complex hydrographic schemes have been constructed over the centuries, although these efforts have often been tragically thwarted by devastating floods.

The delta region, constantly shrouded in spirals of fog, is the true queen of the area. The Po Delta is a magical spot, fortunately still partly unspoiled, though menaced by a tourist industry attracted by the idea of the huge profits expected to be generated by a controversial park scheme. This "water province" is also beloved of cinema directors, especially the great Roberto Rossellini, who shot one of the most gripping scenes of partisan warfare in the last episode of Paisà there. Michelangelo Antonioni also celebrated Polesine in The Outcry, a tragic love story which was being filmed in the winter of 1956 when the Po burst its banks and displayed all its terrible brute force, dictating its own terms to the director and forcing him to make cuts in the script. This friendly river, yet at times so disquieting and hostile, has left its mark on the people of Polesine.

200 top and top center The Delta area holds some surprises in store for nature lovers. In addition to the sedentary and migratory wild life, there are also fish-farms, which exploit large stretches of briny water to breed mollusks.

200 bottom center Fishing is one of the major sources of income in the Delta area. This photo shows a typical fisherman's cottage.

200 bottom The low herbaceous vegetation, characterized by marsh samphire, sea-lavender, and reeds, is typical of these marshy areas of the Po Delta close to the sea.

200-201 A lovely sunset in the Po Delta. The sun sends out its last gleams of fire before drowning in the water, revealing the outlines of the isolated huts used to store fishing gear.

However much they may suffer, they can rarely tear themselves away from this wildly beautiful spot. The best way of getting to know the river is by boat, meditating on the skilled gestures of the elderly boatmen, the silence of the area and the incredible charm bestowed on it by the flora and fauna, the latter often being the only constant companion in these remote districts. Towns and cities are scattered all around, such as Rovigo, the agricultural capital of Polesine, which also has an important cultural heritage as witnessed by the Accademia dei Concordi, Lendinara, and finally Adria. It's hard to imagine when visiting this small town that long ago, under Greek occupation, it was so important as to be considered the main trading center in the Po Valley. Then the Etruscans arrived, followed by the Romans, who ennobled it with their presence, and it became such an important town that its name was given to the Adriatic Sea, now some 12 miles away from Adria

because of the continual advance of the delta. These lands are imbued with magic. While watching one of their fiery sunsets it is easy to understand why the myth of Phaeton was set here. Phaeton stole the chariot of the sun, but in his youthful inexperience he was unable to control the reins of the prancing horses, and burned the Earth and the Sky. The solemn Zeus intervened, and hurled the imprudent charioteer into the River Po. His sisters, the Heliades, mourned his death, and moved the gods so much that they turned them into poplars out of compassion. Those same trees still offer generous shade to the incurable romantics who walk these streets, day-dreaming of the ancient fables and musing on the profound significance of the old adage "The Po is born where the scent of the sea is in the air." Recalling the myth and the proverb, we finally realize that the palpable sweetness of these lovely wild spots has all the passion of an ancient lament behind it.

PADUA AND THE BRENTA RIVIERA, TREVISO AND THE "JOYFUL REGION"

202 top This delightful country residence, built by Andrea Palladio for the nobleman Leonardo Emo at Fanzolo, in the Treviso region, is a classic mansion with porticoed canopy roofs at the sides.

202-203 Immersed in lush vegetation, Villa Foscari, traditionally known as "La Malcontenta," is one of the gems built by Palladio on the banks of the River Brenta.

203 top Villa Nani
Mocenigo, widely believed
to have been designed by
Vincenzo Scamozzi, stands
on the banks of the
Canalbianco at Canda, in
the province of Rovigo.

Leaving Fusina behind us after taking our leave of Venice, we follow the road that leads, as in the past, towards the "delights of the River Brenta." Of course, we can no longer enjoy the pleasure of embarking on the burchiello, a little river boat decorated with mirrors, carvings, and paintings, which used to be towed across the lagoon to the mainland by a tug and then pulled by horses led along the towpath. In Arcadia in Brenta ovvero la melanconia sbandita (Arcadia in Brenta, Or Melancholy Banished), Giovanni Sagredi describes the craft as "a mobile room, a floating apartment."

Carlo Goldoni gives a similar description, set at a time when the Venetians of the ancient Republic longed for summer and autumn holidays, and those who could afford them swarmed merrily to spend their days of leisure amid the amusements that the magnificent villas built along the "placid river" reserved for the idle rich. But what delights were in store for the "young gentlemen," the last squanderers of what was often a meager inheritance, already laid waste by generations of spendthrifts? Father Goldoni acts as our guide, explaining the motivation behind all these desires - luxury, opulence, and the vices of gambling and love - which while on vacation could be enjoyed with greater freedom than in the strictly supervised drawing rooms of Venetian villas, where tyrannical fathers, virtuous mothers, and a swarm of servants always willing to act the spy meant that privacy was non-existent.

Although this was the reigning way of life as the libertine period of the early eighteenth century drew to a close, life in the sixteenth century must have been very different, as we are reminded by the magnificent Villa Foscari, known as La Malcontenta (Villa of Discontent). A pretty young woman, one Elisabetta Dolfin, who had proved rather too fond of worldly pleasures in licentious Venice, had been severely punished for her lascivious behavior by being shut away in that gilded cage, designed by Andrea Palladio for brothers Nicolò and Luigi Foscari. Set amid a profusion of greenery, where the fronds of the weeping willows that bow gently down to the waters of a loop of a navigable canal conceal just enough of the magnificent architecture to frame it, the villa can only be compared with the garden of Eden. However, as a Venetian proverb has it, "being all alone is no fun, not even in paradise." This romantic story has become legendary, and a portrait of a woman by Giambattista Zelotti in one of the frescoed rooms of the villa is widely believed to depict Elisabetta.

All that luxury was not enough to dispel the cravings of a young woman addicted to pleasure. What a waste, yet one can't help feeling envious; those ancient Venetians certainly lived well!. Another princely mansion, Villa Widmann Rezzonico Foscari, stands just outside Mira. Here, the architecture is more modest and the architect is unknown. The original nucleus dating from 1719, perhaps designed by Tirali, has been rebuilt on numerous occasions. The villa is impressive, with its great French rococo ballroom decorated with frescoes framed by stucco work, and the magnificent paintings remind the visitor that the Widmanns, noble Carinthian merchants, were related to the Rezzonico family, one of whose members, the future Pope Clement XIII, spent happy days in the villa as a cardinal, unaware that one day he would be weighed down with the cares of the Papacy.

A few miles beyond Dolo, just outside Stra, stands the most attractive and magnificent villa on the Brenta Riviera: Villa Pisani, known as La Nazionale. At the height of the decadence of Venice, in 1735, Alvise Pisani had been elected Doge, and the mansion, commissioned from Gerolamo Frigimelica and continued after the architect's death by Francesco Maria Preti, was almost finished.

The building is truly impressive; the interior consists of 114 rooms frescoed by the best artists of the period, including Ricci, Zais, and Zuccarelli, while the Apotheosis of the Pisani Family in the central hall was painted by the great Giambattista Tiepolo. Famous guests who have stayed at the villa include Napoleon, Maria Luigia of Parma, Maximilian of Hapsburg, Tsar Alexander I, Vittorio

Emanuele II of Savoy and, in 1934, Hitler and Mussolini. Huge grounds with stables and fishponds and the "frescoed house" on the hill, welcome visitors, but the great attraction of the villa is its maze, a mysterious route running between box hedges, a source of amusement designed by a whimsical gardener for the enjoyment of ladies and gentlemen during the era of beauty spots, powder, and crinolines. It has now been restored to its original splendor, but when D'Annunzio described it in Fuoco, it had run wild, and the rusty, squeaking gate led to a tangled excess of vegetation.

However, in that neglected state it was perhaps better able to liberate the hero's sensual capacity, his sensitivity towards the spirits of nature, and his eventual communion with forest life. Real mazes and the mazes of the soul: a magical coincidence.

204 top One of the 114 rooms furnished with exquisite eighteenth-century pieces which form the gigantic Villa Pisani complex in Stra is named after Bacchus.

204 bottom The Pisani family, which had achieved an important position among the Venetian nobility, commissioned Tiepolo to paint the Apotheosis of the family on the ballroom ceiling.

204-205 With its huge grounds, stables, and the famous maze, immortalized in D'Annunzio's novel Fuoco, the majestic Villa Pisani, known as "La Nazionale," at Stra on the Brenta Riviera, is a mansion worthy of a Doge.

The father of Italian psychoanalysis, Cesare Musatti, was born just a stone's throw away from this enchanting, romantic spot, and on the very same day, September 21, 1897, Sigmund Freud passed by on his way to Venice. On the same day he expounded on his new theory in a letter to Fliess, which is why Musatti jokingly called psychoanalysis "my twin sister." Be that as it may, there are really too many coincidences, and the real or imaginary labyrinth becomes ever more intricate!

Leaving the magic of the Brenta Riviera behind, Padua, City of the Saint, lies ready to welcome. Ancient mythology has been invoked to account for the foundation of Padua, which antedates Rome, and the choice fell on the Trojan Antenor, presumably a character of little virtue, because in accordance with a late post-Homeric interpretation, Dante gave his name to one of the circles in the lower inferno to which traitors to their country were assigned (Inferno, XXXII, 88). Padua was later given a new aura of respectability as the City of the Saint, the saint in question being the best loved in the world, Saint Anthony of Lisbon, who was so impressed by the simplicity and humility of the first Franciscan monks that he serenely embarked on the career of preacher, and ended his days in this remote spot before passing on to celestial beatitude in heaven.

Padua, a university town with an illustrious academic history, is a city of "great scholars" according to tradition, but also fond of a joke. The university is called the "Bo" (the ox) by the locals, because it stands on the site of an ancient inn that bore the sign of an ox.

The university was founded in 1222, and Galileo Galilei gave lectures freely there before being lured away by the more attractive financial offer made by Grand Duke Cosimo II. Unfortunately, there were some very unpleasant surprises in store for him when it came to freedom of thought.

208 top The Law Courts were once housed in Palazzo della Ragione, in this huge hall with its magnificent roof shaped like the hull of a ship.

Albertino Mussato, Alvise Cornaro, and Angelo Beolco, better known as Ruzante, are some of the most famous graduates of the university, that great melting pot of Paduan culture. In more recent times, playwright Carlo Goldoni obtained a law degree from the university, although he preferred theatrical to legal oratory. Another student, Giacomo Casanova, while attending law school there, had not yet decided between an ecclesiastical career and the libertine vocation to which he eventually devoted body and soul with truly laudable dedication.

Padua is a city of art, offering a wealth of paintings and architecture, from the Roman Patavium, an opulent and densely populated city of the Roman Empire, the remains of which are to be found everywhere, to the medieval Palazzo della Ragione and the beloved Basilica of the Saint, built to house the precious remains of Saint Anthony. Later graced by Giotto's prestigious frescoes in the chapel dedicated by Enrico Scrovegni to the memory of his father (who was included among the usurers in Dante's Inferno) in 1305, Padua became a center of the arts in the fourteenth century.

208-209 The walls of the Great Hall of Padua's Palazzo della Ragione are covered with fresco cycles featuring a mixture of sacred and profane themes, including the astrological series inspired by the writings of famous doctor and astrologer Pietro d'Abano.

209 top The Romanesque-Gothic Eremitani Church, which was seriously damaged by bombing in 1944, was rebuilt to restore at least fragments of the magnificent frescoes painted by Mantegna.

209 bottom The huge fruit and vegetable market has always been held in Piazza delle Erbe and under the porticoes of Palazzo della Ragione.

210 top The interior of St. Anthony's Basilica, divided into a nave and two aisles, has a Latin cross layout. Galleries run along the walls, and the interior space is dominated by the huge vaults of the domes.

210 bottom Pilgrims from all over the world flock to St. Anthony's Basilica to pay homage to St. Anthony of Lisbon, who rests in peace for all eternity in Padua.

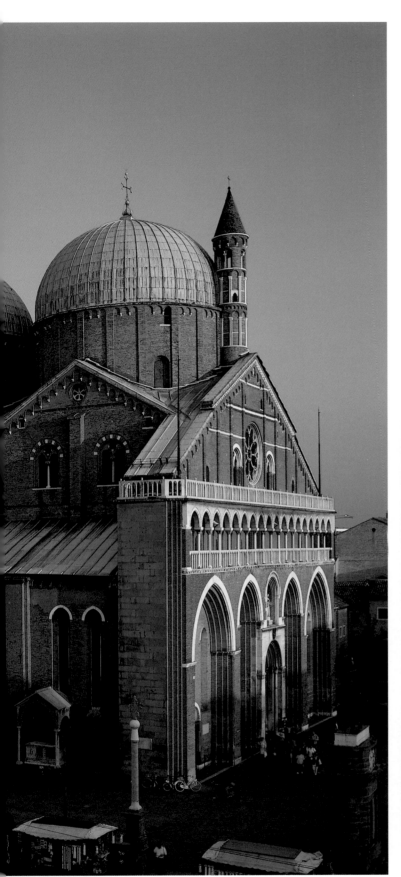

However, it was Tuscan artist Giusto de' Menabuoi and above all Donatello who brought to life the miracles of Saint Anthony in the reliefs on the high altar of the Basilica. Donatello also sculpted the equestrian statue of Erasmo da Narni, known as Gattamelata, in homage to a military leader who had valiantly served the Republic of Venice, which still ruled Padua. Andrea Mantegna did some of his best work in the Eremitani Church, but much of it was destroyed in a devastating bombing raid in 1944. However, the Ovetari Chapel still contains at least one sample of his work.

The city offers nature lovers the oldest Botanical Garden in the world. It was founded in 1545 by resolution of the Senate of the Veneto Republic to grow medicinal plants, and exotic plants from various parts of the world were added over the centuries, until it became a center of cultivation and research of enviable international prestige.

210-211 St. Anthony's Basilica is an architectural complex featuring an astonishing blend of Romanesque and Gothic elements and even Islamic style, as in the bell towers, which strongly resemble minarets.

211 The high altar of the Presbytery of St. Anthony's Basilica, designed by Donatello, was totally rebuilt in the late nineteenth century. The restructuring work was controversial, but at least the bronzes by Donatello and his school were preserved.

Padua is best appreciated on foot, strolling past the noisy stalls of the markets in Piazza delle Erbe, sizing up Piazza dei Signori from the porticoes, or visiting one of the biggest piazzas in Italy, Prato della Valle (Valley Meadow), which is surrounded by an elliptical canal and sits on the site where the Roman amphitheater once stood.

However, the true atmosphere of the city can be breathed in the famous "doorless" Café Pedrocchi, which was built in the style of a Neoclassical temple.

213 bottom *Giotto painted his Last Judgement, which covers the entire entrance wall of the Scrovegni Chapel, in rich colors, in accordance with traditional iconography.*

212-213 and 213 top
The simple, aisle-less structure of the Scrovegni Chapel in Padua is entirely covered by Giotto's masterpiece depicting stories of Mary and Christ, divided into three strips and 38 panels.

212 bottom left *Giotto's intense vision of the Flight to Egypt is set in a landscape dominated by a pyramid-shaped spur of rock, against which the protagonists stand out.*

212 bottom right *On this panel in the Chapel, Giotto depicts the episode in which an angel announces the future birth of the Virgin Mary to her father, Joachim, in a dream.*

There, in the cold silence of the marble interior, possibly in contrast with the jesting young voice of a new graduate giving his first mock public speech in front of the café in accordance with custom, the visitor begins to enter into the spirit of this singular city, whose emblem is oddness and gaiety.

With his usual elegance and erudition Toni Cibotto, the famous author, told me the popular saying which gives an illuminating perception of the character of the city: "Padua, the city that has a café with no doors, a meadow with no grass, and a saint with no name."

Because of the traffic and pollution that besiege all big cities, and Padua in particular, those fine, clear days that reveal the miracle of the nearby Euganean Hills are becoming increasingly rare.

The durable trachyte that paves many cities used to be quarried in these hills, and their volcanic origin is demonstrated by the numerous hot springs from which emerge rivers of miracle-working mud, essential for curing arthritis and rheumatism, that has made the fortune of well-known local spas like Abano, Montegrotto, and Battaglia Terme.

With their conical and rounded shapes, covered with copses, locust trees, and hazel groves, the Euganean hills, named after a population that lived in the area in ancient times, have existed since time immemorial, a reassuring, cheering sight.

It must be these delightful features which have made them the home of poets, such as the tired old Petrarch, who preferred to spend the last years of his old age among the olive groves and vineyards of the picturesque, quiet town of Arquà, which now bears his revered name. In Ugo Foscolo's Jacopo Ortis, the bad mood of the hero, "angry with the deities of the fatherland" and with Napoleon for having ceded Venice to Austria, is dispelled by the fresh air of these hills, and at least for a little while he is reconciled to the world by his tender love for the beautiful Teresa.

214 top In a stretch of countryside in the Treviso Marches, the medieval tower of Roganzuolo Castle keeps watch over the plain. The castles, fortresses, and walled towns of Veneto, monuments of fear that are still perfectly preserved, constitute one of the many attractions of this region.

214 bottom This lovely view of the Alpago Pre-Alps, a high wall between the Piave and Cellina rivers features a profusion of greenery and nature. The Veneto Pre-Alpine area features mountains of altitudes ranging between 2300 and 7300 feet.

214-215 Silence reigns supreme in the endless vineyards near Combai, known for producing an excellent, light, sparkling Prosecco. Veneto offers many oases of nature and peace, together with the artificial paradises of the palate along its wine and food routes.

216-217 *Because of its strategic position, Montagnana was given stout medieval walls, which have withstood the ravages of time. They still protect the town today for a length of more than a mile, giving it an austere look.*

However, he also expresses his indignation at the appalling neglect of Petrarch's house, reduced to a heap of ruins overrun by nettles and weeds. Fortunately, his poetic plea was heard, recorded for posterity, and granted.

Tranquility of soul and mind is also to be found in the Benedictine monastery of Praglia, where the monks still live in a timeless age, tending medicinal plants or restoring precious manuscripts.

However, this peace visibly clashes with the numerous remains of turreted and walled cities like Monselice Castle, residence of the fierce Ezzelino da Romano, Este Castle, and especially the endless medieval brick walls which have defended Montagnana for centuries and constitute one of the best examples of ancient fortifications in Europe.

217 top right Castelfranco, the birthplace of Giorgione, is distinguished from the other walled towns of Veneto by its castle, whose construction was ordered by Treviso. This photo shows St. Mark's lion and the clock on the Civic Tower.

217 bottom The unusual Villa Giustinian (now known as Villa Ciani-Bassetti) at Roncade was built towards the end of the fifteenth century in the form of a medieval castle.

War and peace, tranquil abbeys and lonely hermitages or the distant sound of war trumpets; all the charm and incredible appeal of these lovely spots is summed up in this obvious contradiction.

When Petrarch wrote of "clear, fresh, sweet waters," he was inspired by the crystal-clear River Sorga near Valchiusa, but the same poetic impression is received when standing on Dante's Bridge at Treviso and looking down, as the stone tablet says, at the spot "where Sile and Cagnan come together" (Paradiso, IX, 49). Although the River Cagnan is now called the Botteniga, Treviso still remains the "city of water," with its numerous canals and karstic springs.

218-219 This picturesque view of the porticoes overlooking Canale dei Buranelli shows one of the loveliest spots in Treviso.

218 bottom The sixteenth-century walls and monumental city gates give Treviso the severe look of an ancient medieval town.

219 Treviso's amazing labyrinth of canals, and the confluence of the River Botteniga (called the Cagnano in ancient times) with the crystal-clear waters of the River Sile, have justly earned it the nickname of "city of water."

220 left The Chapter-house of the Dominicans in the former Monastery of St. Nicolò in Treviso is decorated with frescoes by Tomaso da Modena, famous because they constitute the first documented evidence of the use of spectacles.

It's a medieval city, a painted town, where the façades of the houses display the faded remnants of gaudy ancient tapestries, with coats of arms and ornaments to demonstrate their kinship to noble families that are now wholly extinct.

Piazza dei Signori and Palazzo dei Trecento recall medieval splendors that have fallen into oblivion for centuries. These roads were once traveled by dashing squires and seraphic Dominican monks, like those humorously portrayed by the great illustrator Tomaso da Modena in the chapter-house of San Nicolò, absorbed in their studies, with eyes so weakened by long and sometimes tedious reading that they required the aid of the first spectacles recorded in history.

Treviso emerges from the waters like an island, as does the delightful fish market in its fairytale setting. Not far away, the vanes of derelict watermills keep turning impassively, while the waters flow quietly all around. These placid waters are disturbed only by a trout suddenly darting to the surface, or the quacking of a mallard as it crossly follows an over-impertinent companion, while from the height of its mute, regal inscrutability a swan, with sinuously elegant

220-221 The busy Piazza dei Signori, with its welcoming porticoes and elegant shops and cafés, is the showplace of Treviso and a popular meeting place with its inhabitants.

221 40 panels painted by Tomaso da Modena depict the most famous personalities of the Dominican order, absorbed in reading in their lonely cells.

movements, observes the quiet, eternal flow of the river. Yet modernity also puts in an appearance here, in the scintillating windows of the luxurious shops under the welcoming porticoes of the main street called Calmaggiore.

The girls strolling down the street are proverbially beautiful, the very same girls who inspired film director Pietro Germi to expose the subtle erotic subterfuges and hypocrisy of seemingly respectable married folk in Signore e Signori.

Treviso is also the capital of what used to be known as the "Joyful Region," and it certainly deserves that epithet, if only for the geographical beauty of its districts and the fertile land on which towns like Conegliano are built, surrounded by vineyards famed for their white prosecco. Castelvecchio (the old castle), built in the tenth century and included under the rule of Verona and Venice, stands in the walled town of that medieval fortress, which has existed for centuries, and still retains traces of its noble past.

Conegliano was the birthplace of Cima, who ennobled the town with his magical brush. Other ancient towns also produced some great painters, like Castelfranco Veneto, the birthplace of Giorgione, where more city walls and another defensive castle can be seen. However, it is at Asolo, the home of Caterina Cornaro, Queen of Cyprus, where we really become immersed in history. Its severe fortress dominates the area, offering a delightful view over the hills and lush vegetation from which Asolo emerges supreme.

It is imbued with an incredible charm, which is why it was chosen as their home by many famous personalities such as Bembo, Giorgione, Eleonora Duse, and Robert Browning. Even the unusually tame-looking lion lying on the great fountain seems to feel very much at home here, and has nothing of the arrogant, aggressive pose typical of its counterparts throughout the dominions of Veneto, which are always portrayed standing, looking proudly ahead.

223 bottom The fortress, with the encircling walls descending towards the castle, offers a severe image of placid Asolo, nestling in a landscape that exudes peace and quiet. The humanistic court of noblemen and artists with which Caterina Cornaro, Queen of Cyprus, surrounded herself restored the peace she needed after the dramatic family events she had experienced, and changed the face of this delightful town for all time.

224 top The real genius of Palladio lay in the skill with which he blended his architectural creations, consisting of porticoes, nyphaeum, fishponds, dovecotes, and gardens, with the magnificent geographical position of Maser, molded by nature.

224 center Veronese lavished all his genius on the cross-vaults of Villa Barbaro, inventing a rustic concert with musicians, singers, pages, and curious little girls peeping out from behind imitation doors.

224 bottom The large, well-lit rooms of Villa Barbaro display the pictorial genius of Paolo Veronese, who was commissioned to paint the frescoes, while Alessandro Vittoria made the stucco mouldings and the numerous sculptures.

225 Villa Barbaro, in Maser, was commissioned from Palladio in 1560 by Daniele Barbaro, Patriarch of Aquileia, and his brother Marcantonio, Ambassador of the Venetian Republic.

226-227 This field of sunflowers in the Treviso region is a blaze of color.

We certainly can't fault the artist's choice. Everything here is conducive to the serenity of the soul and gaiety of spirit.

If we also want to find art, we need only walk a little way to visit Villa Barbaro at Maser, where Andrea Palladio, Paolo Veronese, and Alessandro Vittoria created a true miracle. Daniele, Patriarch of Aquileia, and his brother Marcantonio Barbaro, Ambassador of the Republic of Venice, were learned humanists and erudite scholars, and their villa speaks for itself. It was designed by Palladio in accordance with the rules of harmonic proportions he himself laid down: "A city should be none other than a great house, and conversely, a house should be a small city." The astute Barbaro family were very far-sighted; only art could make them immortal, and they are all still there to welcome us. Marcantonio's beloved wife Giustiniana Giustiniani, portrayed accompanied by a nurse, leans over the balcony, while all round, nature plays the daintiest of minuets in and out of the imitation pergolas, and the painted landscapes seem to break through the walls. In other portraits, a page spies on visitors from behind a door, and a curious, smiling little girl who has come to hide in this very room suddenly realizes she has been discovered, almost seeming to protest that the intrusion has disturbed her game.

Leaving her there in peace, silently playing her childish games, she has been eternally condemned to this happy fate by the hand of an unusual and very whimsical artist.

228 top left Vicenza, city of the arts, offers numerous opportunities and places of rare beauty in which everyone can refine and stimulate their own talents in an endless variety of styles and inspired combinations.

228 top right This photo shows a detail of the façade of the Church of San Vincenzo in Vicenza's Piazza dei Signori, with its unmistakable bell tower.

VICENZA, VERONA, AND LAKE GARDA

228-229 Piazza dei Signori, with the majestic Palladian Basilica and two elegant columns on the east side, one ornamented with St. Mark's lion and the other with the statue of the Redeemer, is the hub of Vicenza's daily life.

Vicenza and Andrea Palladio are inseparable. Palladio, the architect from Padua, had the pulsating heart of an entire city as the testing ground for his genius, but he also had the luck to encounter a rich caste of ambitious Vicenza men who were constantly competing with Venice and happy to loosen their purse-strings if it meant making a good impression. Vicenza already had its Gothic Ca' d'oro, but without the Grand Canal to reflect it, it could hardly compete with the buildings of Venice.

Vicenza also boasted the unique, picturesque Casa Pigafetta, in which Gothic, Spanish, and early Renaissance architecture are extravagantly combined. However, as the family motto of Antonio Pigafetta, the navigator who accompanied Magellan's voyage round the world, puts it, "There's no rose without a thorn," and for the people of Vicenza, envy was a real thorn in the flesh. If Vicenza is still counted among the great cities of art today, it is largely due to those ancient philanthropists and to Andrea Palladio.

Yet Palladio's relationship with the city was uneasy to begin with, and clearly full of suspicion. In fact, although the architect had brilliantly resolved the problem of restoring the Gothic palazzo, with its magnificent marble facing and serliana windows, in an outstanding design presented to the High Council in 1546, the work was postponed because the city's administrators decided to submit the plan to the judgment of the entire community. The arch was meanwhile built of wood and abandoned for nearly two years, until the resolution was finally passed by 99 votes to 17 on April 11, 1549.

Palladio made his name with the monumental Basilica in Piazza dei Signori, his first public building, but his fame and fortune came thanks to his benefactor, Giangiorgio Trissino.

Andrea, son of miller Pietro della Gondola and his wife, nicknamed "lame Marta," would never have achieved much success if it hadn't been for his encounter with that famous man of letters, who was a veritable talent scout. Andrea, "son of Pietro of Padua," took the name of Palladio, in accordance with the rhetoric of the humanistic culture and custom of the day, in gratitude to the man who had introduced him to the beauties of classical art in Rome.

229 top Palazzo della Ragione, universally known by the name of "Basilica," was the first public building to be designed in Vicenza by Palladio, who brilliantly solved the problem by enclosing the existing Gothic structure in elegant classical loggias.

229 bottom This photo shows the monumental stage of the Olympic Theater, the oldest surviving indoor theater, which was built by Palladio for the Academy of the same name. It was inaugurated on March 3, 1585 with a performance of Sophocles' Oedipus Rex.

230-231 *Vicenza is situated in a delightful position at the foot of the Berici Mountains, embellished by the confluence of the Retrone and Bacchiglione rivers which surround the city.*

Palladio amply repaid his debt of gratitude not only to his illustrious discoverer, but to all his less prominent fellow citizens.

Palladio and the rational forms of his buildings are ever-present in Vicenza, from the Loggia del Capitanato to Palazzo Chiericati, which now houses the Civic Museum, from Palazzo Marcantonio Thiene to his masterpiece, the Olimpico Theater, which was his last great work. The theater is so magical that although it was built in haste like many Renaissance theaters and perhaps not destined to survive for long after the production of Sophocles' Oedipus Rex during the 1585 carnival, it still stands today as an artistic testament, the glorious beauty of its Vitruvian forms still intact. The only arbitrary license that has been taken with it is represented by the trompe l'oeuil perspectives of the permanent wooden sets built by Vincenzo Scamozzi, who took over the supervision of the work after Palladio's death.

230 bottom and 231 Some wonderful views can be seen from the ancient bridges over the River Bacchiglione, such as the impressive verdigris-covered roof of the Basilica, which towers over the surrounding buildings.

232-233 The Sanctuary of Mount Berico, on a shady green hillside overlooking Vicenza, offers a magnificent view of the city.

But it was in villas like the famous Villa Capra, known all over the world as La Rotonda that Palladio expressed the best of his ability.

Here, the architect fell in love with the landscape, and saw the need for harmony between ancient forms and nature, as he wrote in his Quattro Libri dell'Architettura.

He was certainly aided by the site, a delightful spot on the top of a small hill from which an outstanding view can be seen. The hills all round, covered with lush vineyards, appear to the artist's eye like a great stage offering views on every side.

This is why the villa has four temple-style elevations with wide steps to demonstrate the sense of holiness that emanates from that landscape, to which no face can be shown other than the unique, palpitating features of the god of nature who lives there. Rational classical forms are married with the delights of the surrounding environment in a true natural theater, which meant designing buildings in accordance with the rules of harmony laid down by the ancients.

Apollo and Dionysus represent reason and irrationality, as in love, where the imprudent irresponsibility of the lover contrasts with the subtle strategy of the seducer, who weaves his fine web with an ever tighter net. That's why Joseph Losey located his Don Giovanni in this setting, which is both natural and artificial at the same time. The same face appears on all sides and everything revolves around it, as in Mozart's opera.

It makes no difference whether Don Giovanni is present or absent: everyone talks about him and his amazing prowess as an shameless rake. The charm that emanates from the peaceful surrounding landscape is equally irresistible. The greenery of the Berici mountains seems to have been specifically designed to act as a backdrop to Arcadia, and the two Tiepolos, father and son, did some of their best work in the nearby Villa Valmarana. Giambattista Tiepolo painted his epic and chivalrous cycle, ranging from The Iliad to Orlando Furioso, from The Aeneid to Jerusalem Delivered, apparently more interested in "women, courtesies, and loves" than in "knights, arms, and audacious feats." In the guest quarters, Giandomenico Tiepolo, free of his father's oppressive influence, depicted his beloved carnival costumes, mountebanks, Commedia dell'Arte characters, and the marvels of the cosmorama or the magic lantern of the "New World." With deft brushstrokes he sometimes portrayed the Venetians under the subtle spell of carnival time, refreshing their spirits by taking a holiday among country people gathered around a fragrant table, or enjoying a well-deserved siesta, and sometimes invented a fantastic Orient, based on the writings of Marco Polo and the fairytale atmospheres of Carlo Gozzi.

234 Villa Valmarana ai Nani, situated in an enviable position on the road leading to Mount Berico, is famous for the cycle of frescoes painted by Giambattista Tiepolo soon after his return from Würzburg.

235 top left Villa Capra, known as "La Rotonda," is the most famous building designed by Andrea Palladio. The sun can be enjoyed all day long at the top of this delightful knoll, where the four identical pronaos façades have a precise astronomical orientation.

235 center left Villa Chiericati-Lambert at Longa di Schiavon in the province of Vicenza, which was built in 1560 but later given a new, Neoclassical façade, contains frescoes painted by a disciple of Paolo Veronese.

235 bottom left This fresco in Villa Valmarana ai Nani, painted by Giambattista Tiepolo, portrays Aeneas presenting Cupid to Dido in the guise of his son Ascanius.

235 top right Villa Valmarana ai Nani, was built by Antonio Muttoni in 1669.

Piazza dei Signori, Verona,
where Ugo Zannoni's famous
monument to Dante of 1865
stands, feature a wide variety
of styles which blend
perfectly with one another.

The province of Vicenza has bitter memories of
World War I, which are hard to eradicate from a
population that suffered terribly under occupation.
However, the noisy reunions of the veterans and new
recruits to the Alpine troops seem to have repressed
the pain and suffering experienced during the long
period of trench warfare, especially after the rout at
Caporetto, when the defense of the River Piave and
Monte Grappa was entrusted to 18-year-old recruits.
It's enough to hear a choir singing "We'll Shake
Hands On Bassano Bridge" over a glass of grappa,
the democratic queen that does not disdain the
humblest table and "burns up your troubles"
according to the country adage, to witness the
triumph of good humor and conviviality.

Sitting around a massive table in the oldest grappa
tavern in Italy, founded in 1779, before an
interminable row of copper vats on the Alpine Troops
Bridge at Bassano del Grappa and watching the
tumultuous waters of the River Brenta flowing
beneath the window, we understand that although
war, devastation, bombing, and floods have done their
worst, they could not prevail against the stubborn
will of these people.

They have learned, at a price, how to survive
beyond the time allowed by fate, just like that wooden
bridge designed by Palladio with its magical row of
wooden pillars, which has often been destroyed, but
always been rebuilt "just as it used to be." Marostica,
not far from Bassano, was once ruled by the Della
Scala family, and its two castles, the upper castle
clinging to the hillside and the lower castle
overlooking the piazza named after it, suggest that
the medieval town was forced by bellicose neighbors
to build impregnable defensive ramparts. However,
disputes, especially over affairs of the heart, were
sometimes easily solved without bloodshed, perhaps
over a chessboard, in accordance with a tradition
recently rediscovered among the dusty yellowed
parchments in the castle archives.

The ancient document contains an order originally
issued by Cangrande della Scala, and later confirmed
by the Doge of Venice, and strictly prohibited duels
between noblemen and knights "in memory of the
unhappy lovers Lady Juliet Capulet and Lord Romeo

236 center The Loggia del
Consiglio in Piazza dei
Signori is a masterpiece
of the Verona Renaissance
period which, according to
tradition, was built by
Dominican monk Fra'
Giocondo towards the end of
the fifteenth century to house
the City Council.

236 bottom The Scala
Arches, a detail of which
is shown here, are the
monumental tombs of
the lords of Verona, and
considered a masterpiece
of Gothic funerary art.

236-237 In Roman times, the Forum stood in Verona's Piazza delle Erbe. Now, as shown in this aerial photo, it is the site of a busy market selling fruit, vegetables, flowers, and plants.

237 bottom The crenellated Scala bridge over the River Adige, with its three red brick arches, which was seriously damaged during the Second World War and perfectly rebuilt, gives access to the Castelvecchio defensive complex.

Montague," increased the penalties for disobedience, and ordered that the challenge "should be fought out over a noble game of chess."

Cangrande, a historical character, and the tragic story of the two lovers, the "poor sacrifices of enmity," which is such a romantic legend that it has almost gained factual status, are typical of Verona, a city where history and fantasy are intermingled more than anywhere else. This colonia augusta contains some well-preserved Roman ruins, including a theater used for modern performances and an arena where grand operas are staged today, with "celestial Aida" and the triumphal marches of Radames taking the place of combat between men and wild beasts and mock naval battles. Arias instead of gladiators: magical Verona could not ask for more.

Verona also offers the spectacular Castelvecchio and the River Adige which flows placidly under the arches of the crenellated Scaligero bridge, from which visitors can look down onto the water as they stroll, imagining the city's medieval past and daydreaming

of ladies, knights, and courtly love. In the Church of Santa Anastasia, Pisanello's fine brushstrokes depict holy warriors with their steeds caparisoned in a more festive than warlike way, liberating towns from terrible fire-breathing dragons, and impassive princesses with angelic profiles who seem to be more concerned about keeping their elaborate hairstyles in place than about the fate of the curly-haired, effeminate blond knight who could not look less like Saint George.

238 top left This photo shows one of the odd "hunchbacks" of Sant'Anastasia which support the holy water stoups. According to tradition, they are effigies of millers from the Adige watermills.

238 bottom left St. Zeno's Gate is covered with 48 bronze panels depicting episodes from the life of St. Zeno, allegorical figures, and Biblical stories.

238 top right The Romanesque cloister of St. Zeno is built round a grassy area. It has a large portico with red marble coupled columns supporting raised and pointed arches.

238 bottom right The magnificent Gothic structure of Sant'Anastasia contains the famous Pisanello fresco St. George Saving The Princess. This photo shows the interior of the church.

238-239 San Zeno Maggiore is one of the most magnificent examples of Romanesque architecture in Northern Italy. It was built to house the remains of the Patron Saint of Verona, starting in 1120.

In any case, Saint George is not the patron saint of the city. The ever-surprising Verona sought its saint elsewhere, in Africa, according to tradition, in the dark-skinned Saint Zeno. The church dedicated to St. Zeno is the best example of Romanesque architecture in the whole of northern Italy. In magical Verona a star launched like a meteorite lands unfailingly in the central Piazza Bra every Christmas, causing no damage.

A mixture of history and fantasy is the destiny of Verona, and the legend of two star-crossed lovers, first immortalized by the fertile pen of Luigi da Porto from Vicenza, persuaded two more authors, first Matteo Bandello and then Shakespeare, to write the most heartbreaking and realistic love story of all time. An inn at 27 Via Cappello was transformed long ago into Juliet's house. Standing under its marble balcony, which makes lovers sigh and evokes romantic nocturnal encounters, disturbed only by the song of the unwelcome lark heralding the imminent dawn which ineluctably separates the lovers, the significance of the words pronounced by the handsome Romeo before leaving his beloved town can be clearly understood:

"There is no world without Verona walls,
But purgatory, torture, hell itself.
Hence-banished is banish'd from the world,
And world's exile is death."

ROMEO AND JULIET, ACT THREE, SCENE THREE

240 top and bottom
This magnificent part of
Palazzo Giusti in Verona
is a delightful spot full of
greenery, fanciful tree shapes,
and mythological statues.

240 center and 241 One of
the loveliest examples of an
Italian-style Renaissance
garden, with pergolas,
fountains, and viewpoints,
can be admired at Palazzo
Giusti in Verona.

242-243 *Verona by night offers some lovely views of palazzi and monuments overlooking the River Adige.*

242 bottom Verona, the home town of star-crossed lovers Romeo and Juliet, immortalized by Shakespeare's tragedy, is one of the most popular places in Italy to get married.

243 left The Gothic complex of Sant'Anastasia and the Lamberti Tower dominate the city once ruled by the La Scala family in this lovely night view.

243 right The Madonna Verona fountain, based on a Roman statue that was moved to the center of Piazza delle Erbe in 1368, has become a symbol of the city over the centuries.

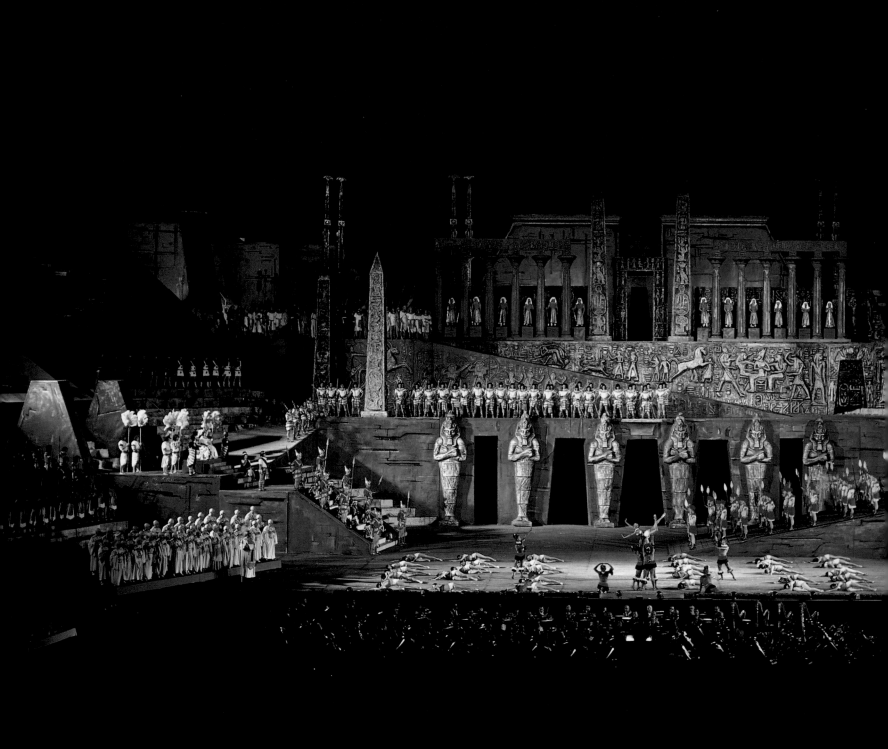

244-245 *Thanks to the magical Arena, one of the few functioning open-air opera theaters in the world, the Verona operatic season attracts a regular crowd of opera lovers every summer.*

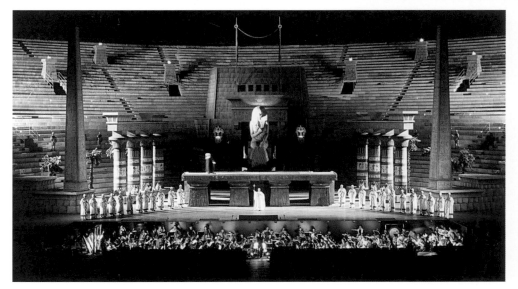

244 bottom There is no better venue for Verdi's Aida, with its sumptuous sets, triumphal march, and superb choreography, than the huge stage of the Verona Arena.

245 top and bottom The huge elliptical amphitheater, which dominates Piazza Bra, was built in the first century A.D. for gladiator fights, indicating the importance of Verona in Roman times.

245 center The first season of the Opera Festival, to which Verona's Arena owes its fame, opened on August 10, 1913.

Verona holds more surprises for lovers of nature and the best produce. Soave is a town that truly lives up to its name which means "delightful." Perhaps it was a connoisseur who bestowed this name on the town, who fell in love not only with this peaceful spot (although a fortress and defensive city walls bear witness to a warlike past), but above all with its excellent white wine and the neat vineyards on the hillsides, a potentially more persuasive argument. Excellent vines also abound in the Monti Lessini area, which is a very good place to try Valpolicella. The red marble known as "Verona marble," a highly-prized material of which traces can be seen in many aristocratic buildings all over Veneto, actually comes from Sant'Ambrogio di Valpolicella.

Celebrated in immortal verses from Virgil's Georgics, "Fluctibus et fremitu adsurgens, Benace, marino…" (Benacus... with billowy uproar surging like the main), Lake Garda, was called Benacus by the Romans. It holds many delights in store, such as Peschiera, the site of one of the four ancient fortresses that formed the famous, fearsome Quadrilateral. From there, on a clear day, the lovely Sirmione peninsula can be seen far off, with the Rocca Scaligera jutting out into the heart of the lake.

Sirmione, the birthplace of Catullus, another poet who extolled these lovely spots, lies in Lombardy, because the boundary between the Veneto and Lombardy regions starts here at Peschiera, runs along the lakeside and up across Bardolino and Torri del Benaco to Malcesine, at the foot of Mount Baldo, a town associated with an unpleasant memory described by Goethe in his Italienische Reise.

Goethe was attracted by the castle because of its dominant position jutting out over the sea.

It was wide open, with neither doors nor guards, and he began contentedly drawing the tower and

ruins in preparation for a picturesque landscape. Unfortunately, he was mistaken for a spy in the pay of the Emperor of Austria, and forced to explain himself to the mayor and a group of impertinent onlookers.

However, the author of Faust was not at all dismayed by this adventure, and his first good impression was soon restored.

The undeniable beauty of these shores and those famous verses by Virgil continue to attract visitors, and generation after generation of German tourists have made Malcesine their second home.

246 top The delightful Val di Sogno, a lovely green valley on the Lake Garda road between Cassone and Malcesine, is one of the most popular spots in the area attracting tourists from all over the world.

246 bottom This photo shows the delightful marina of Cassone, a hamlet to the south of Malcesine.

246-247 Baia delle Sirene (Mermaid Bay) at Punta San Vigilio offers one of the most romantic views over Lake Garda.

248-249 Malcesine, the northernmost town in the province of Verona, is a popular resort in summer and winter alike because of its delightful location on the slopes of Mount Baldo.

249 top The real attraction of Malcesine is the castle, perched high above Lake Garda. The keep, which was built in the fourteenth century under the rule of the La Scala family, now houses the city's History Museum.

249 center Malcesine's main source of income is tourism, and the marina, with its famous cafés and hotels, is always crowded with tourists, especially Germans following in the footsteps of Goethe.

249 bottom A cable car, from which breathtaking views can be seen, takes visitors rapidly from the town of Malcesine to Tratto Spino, at an altitude of 5900 feet.

THE DOLOMITES AND THE BELLUNO DISTRICT

250 top The medieval town of Feltre, perched high on a hill, relives its glorious past during the annual Palio (tournament), when residents take part in archery contests and horse races.

250 bottom Auronzo di Cadore, dominated by magnificent Dolomite scenery, is one of the most famous mountain resorts, and one of the greatest attractions of the area is the small lake of Santa Caterina, a long reservoir closed by a dam.

250-251 Belluno, attractively encircled by mountains, looks down on the confluence of the Rivers Ardo and Piave, and constitutes the gateway to the Veneto Dolomites.

We have just left Vittorio Veneto, the furthermost outpost of the Province of Treviso. When the city was formed in 1866 by the merger of two delightful towns, Céneda and Serravalle, it inherited its unimaginative name from Vittorio Emanuele II, then King of Italy, but it is better known for the battle that ended World War I in 1918. Now, we set off on the last stage of our journey across Veneto to visit the famous mountains of the Belluno district.

One place definitely worth a visit is the attractive town of Feltre, which occupies the southernmost part of the Belluno Valley. Rich in art and history, it is also known as the "painted town" because the façades of many of its sixteenth-century palazzi are decorated with colorful frescoes.

The façade of the Diocesan Curia portrays the Battle of Lepanto, while Palazzo della Ragione, with its porticoed loggia, was built to a design by Andrea Palladio. The town is proud of its close ties with Venice, as demonstrated by the traditional pageant held on the first Sunday of August to commemorate its annexation to the Republic of Venice in 1404. During this festival, Feltre relives its glorious past amid knights, ladies, and squires in traditional costume, the sound of trumpets and drums, and a horse race in which riders representing the "four quarters" of the town compete for a purse of 15 gold ducats.

This loyalty is still repaid even today by the regular presence of partygoers from Venice, even though the town is known for its very changeable climate.Nearby Belluno, "Queen of the Piave," is also known as "shining city" according to a dubious Celtic etymology. The capital of the Dolomites stands in a magnificent position, with a tiara of mountains to the north (Mount Serva, Mount Pelf, and the "Bishop's Needle"), the rocky pyramid of Mount Pizzocco to the west, and Mount Nevegal to the south. The confluence of the tortuous, foaming River Piave with the smaller Ardo encircles and embellishes the center of Belluno, a small, welcoming town with a less frenetic pace of life than most Veneto towns.

251 top Nineteenth-century scientist and author Antonio Stoppani used this apt metaphor to describe the enchanting Agordo basin: "Just imagine you're in the middle of the serrated circle of a huge king's crown."

252 top *Cibiana di Cadore is a small town in the Belluno district where the unusual trade of key maker was practiced during the Venetian Republic, exploiting the Ronzéi iron mines.*

252 bottom *Nowadays, Cibiana di Cadore is famous for its murals, a tradition that has been continued to the present day by a group of artists who have decided to bring new life and color to this mountain town.*

Like the others, however, it retains the typical, original layout of the streets and porticoes, which can be seen between Piazza dei Martiri, the central shopping area, where the locals promenade up and down, and Piazza Duomo, the monumental center of the city, with its cathedral, designed by Tullio Lombardo, and the Civic Tower, which recalls the time long ago when the city was ruled by count-bishops. However, Piazza Duomo is dominated by the unusual façade of Palazzo dei Rettori, with its twin mullioned windows and columns recalling the Venetian world, an impression that is reinforced by the clock tower which so ostentatiously resembles the Moorish Clock Tower in St. Mark's Square. True human warmth and some delightful sights are also to be found in the picturesque Piazza del Mercato, with the lovely fountain of San Lucano, the Renaissance palazzi, Loggia de' Ghibellini and the Monte di Pietà (pawnbrokers') building.

Leaving Belluno, in Pieve di Cadore, the birthplace of Titian, the artist's simple wooden house with its typical outer gallery facing the sun has been turned into a museum displaying relics of the artist's life. Titian transferred the delights and lovely colors of that sky to his canvases. As a child, he absorbed its colors and then expressed them through the magic of his art so that they can be shared and enjoyed by all.

The people of Cadore are tough folk, used to hard work and sacrifice. After being ruled by the Lords of Camino and the Counts of the Tyrol, they voted to merge with the Republic of Venice to the cry of Eamus Ad Bonos Venetos (Let's join the good people of Venice!). The first fundamental by-laws for the protection of the woods, the main source of wealth of the whole Cadore community, were passed here at Pieve. "Saint Mark's Wood" was vitally important to Venice, but the availability of timber obviously depended mainly on the possibility of transporting it easily, so the logs were cut down to a convenient size, floated down the Piave and Boite rivers as far as possible, then loaded onto rafts and towed to Venice. These districts are now famous for another type of product, and a modern building on the road leading from Pieve to the nearby Tai di Cadore houses the Eyeglass Museum.

The museum's interesting collection, which comprises over 2000 pairs of spectacles dating from the Middle Ages to the present day, reconstructs the fascinating history of what was originally a simple trade, but has developed in these mountain areas to a highly profitable business whose products are renowned all over the world.

However, the real asset and the true beauty of the Belluno district is to be found in the mountains.

The Dolomites, a wonderful natural amphitheater that emerged from the sea and was forged by the elements, are named after a globe-trotting geologist with the resounding name of Déodat-Guy-Sylvain-Tancrède de Gratet de Dolomieu (1750-1801), who

252-253 *San Pietro di Cadore, which stands amid conifer woods, was one of the main suppliers of wood to the Venetian Republic in days of old.*

253 bottom One of the most famous sons of Pieve, capital of Cadore, was Titian, whose humble birthplace now houses a museum featuring the life and works of the great artist.

254-255 Mount Pelmo, nicknamed "the Cart of the Almighty" because of its truncated cone shape, introduces new arrivals from the plains to the world of the Dolomites with its imperious presence.

254 bottom Santa Fosca is a pretty mountain resort nestling in Val Fiorentina, an oasis of greenery.

255 top The source of the River Piave is on Mount Peralba, at the head of Val Visdende. Before it was diverted, the river flowed into the Venice lagoon after following a long route, carrying valuable loads of timber for the Venetian Republic.

255 bottom Mount Civetta is inextricably linked with the history of the sixth grade on the mountaineering scale of difficulty. Visitors to Alleghe are sure to admire the North-West Face, whose owl shape gives the mountain its name.

256-257 A lovely view of
Mount Cristallo at sunset.
The mountain dominates the
Cortina d'Ampezzo valley
from the north, while one of
the most tortured ice couloirs
in the Dolomites slopes down
to the Cimabanche Pass.

257 top left The high Tofane
mountains above Val
Travenanzes loom over the
Falzarego Pass and represent
its main mountaineering
attraction.

257 bottom left Tofana di
Mezzo, which once witnessed
some dramatic military
ventures, is now reached
from Cortina by a steep cable
car that allows skiers to ski
on the slopes of Ra Valles
until late in the season.

was the first to study the sedimentary rocks collected
in these mountains and to discover their unusual
composition based on a mineral, never previously
classified, which is a double carbonate of calcium and
magnesium.

However, if the scientist is forgiving, the
legendary name of "Pale Mountains" is perhaps
preferable and much more fitting to the eminently
human characteristic of these mountains, with their
pale color and the phenomenon that causes them to
turn slowly from pink to deep purple at sunset.

This spectacle of nature is called enrosadira in the
Engadine dialect, and the term is also to be found in
the most authoritative Italian dictionaries. The air is
pure and rarefied, rendered mild even at the coldest
times of winter by the gentle warmth of the sun
which peeps into the magnificent Ampezzo valley that
contains the exclusive holiday resort of Cortina,
"pearl of the Dolomites.

" The spectacular charm of its magnificent
surroundings, constituted by Mounts Tofane,
Cristallo, Sorapis, Pomagagnon, Croda da Lago, and
Nuvolau, to name but a few, makes it truly unique.

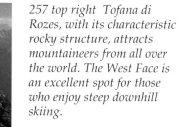

257 top right Tofana di
Rozes, with its characteristic
rocky structure, attracts
mountaineers from all over
the world. The West Face is
an excellent spot for those
who enjoy steep downhill
skiing.

A resort popular with VIPs, business magnates, and show business personalities, it is becoming increasingly inaccessible because of its prohibitive, ever-increasing prices. Sightseers who visit the resort at great expense stroll along Corso Italia, the meeting-place of Cortina's glitterati, hoping to see the stars. This ritual promenade is called the struscio (shuffle), because people are liable to wear their shoes out this way.

All that remains of the ancient Ampezzo families

is a pale recollection in the occasional coat of arms still decorating the façades of the oldest houses or the former Town Hall. The glorious days when blissful peace and quiet could be enjoyed here, far from the traffic, are long gone.

Those were the days of the first famous "Ampezzo Squirrels," the group of climbers inspired by legendary Viennese mountaineer Paul Grohmann, who first started climbing in the Dolomites. His many outstanding followers not only had incredible stamina but also a deep love for the mountains, and never forgot that indescribable sensations must always be accompanied by experience if beauty is not to be paid for with human lives, whereas nowadays, all too many people believe themselves to be experienced guides and tackle the mountains with futuristic equipment, yet lacking the necessary skills.

However, visitors to the Dolomites can satisfy their appetite for nature without risking their skin. Breathtaking views and chocolate-box pictures are imprinted on the waters of Lakes Auronzo and Misurina, which reflect the snow-capped peaks of Mount Cristallino and the Marmarole, the impressive Three Peaks of Lavaredo, and the enchanting, variegated vegetation of the dark woods. Rather like Narcissus, this world is enchanted by its own beauty. The landscape changes: silent hollows alternate with impenetrable thickets where it is easy to imagine that gnomes and elves still dance or play hide-and-seek in the dark cavities of the trees, and watch, silent and ecstatic, the sudden appearance of an acrobatic chamois deer that trots nonchalantly along an inaccessible ledge, or a golden eagle with its menacing shadow plummeting down from the heights where it has built its nest onto some small creature that vainly seeks to escape, while majestic deer graze undisturbed with aristocratic slowness in the Belluno Dolomites National Park.

Here, man has learned to listen to silence, to rejoice in the sacred slow passage of time, and to understand that true civilization has an ancient, primitive soul, very different from the "false, lying gods" of our so-called progress.

262-263 *Terza Grande, Clap Grande, and Mount Siera, which encircle Sappada, make a very interesting nature trek. The names of these little-known groups are influenced by the dialect of nearby Friuli.*

263 top *Cima Piccola, Cima Grande, and Cima Ovest constitute the main part of one of the best-known groups in the Dolomites, the Three Peaks of Lavaredo, which climbers call the "Fantastic Trinity."*

263 center *This photo shows the characteristic haylofts called tabià, which have been part of the mountain landscape of Veneto since time immemorial, with the snow-capped Mount Pelmo in the background.*

263 bottom *Torre del Barancio, Lusy, Romana, Grande, Terza, Quarta, and Inglese are the names of the "Five Towers" (although there are actually more than five peaks, as shown by their names). The highest stands at 525 feet, and they are used as a training ground by the famous mountaineering club called the Cortina Squirrels.*

TRADES AND TRADITIONS

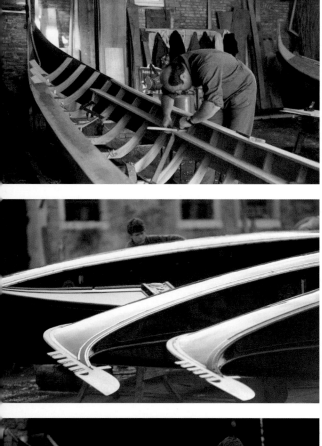

The importance of ancient trades is easy to understand in the Veneto region. Just the fact that Venice, its capital, is a manmade city would have been incomprehensible, and above all impossible, without the work of a host of tradesmen. Secrets jealously preserved for centuries have been handed down from father to son through generations of tradesmen, some from the Italian mainland.

What would Venice be without its stone-masons, without the smiths who tame fire like the divine Hephaestus, and without the skilled carpenters who carve the sinuous shapes and knots of no less than eight types of wood into elegant, asymmetrical gondolas in their boatyards?

Could the magnificent furnishings of the palazzi overlooking the Grand Canal have survived over the centuries without a thriving community of stucco workers, varnishers, wood-carvers, and gilders? Could Murano exist without glass?

Humble sand containing silica, combined with lime and soda which helps it to melt, is transformed in the furnace into an incandescent substance that seems to capture rays of sunlight or harness the glimmerings of twilight in a shapeless blob to which the rapid, skillful gestures of the master glassmaker give body and life. A few deft moves with the pliers, and the structure reveals its soul and releases its colors. The metamorphosis of matter takes place before our astonished gaze: slender, bright, colored, transparent glass is born in all its lightness, symbolizing the fragility of the city that invented this art. Lace has the same fragility.

264 top Gondola construction still follows ancient rules. No less than eight kinds of wood are needed for the body parts and finishing: fir, larch, cherry, walnut, elm, sessile oak, linden, and mahogany.

264 center and bottom The Venetian word squero means the shipyard where gondolas are still built. It derives from squadra (set square), the tool still used by carpenters to make them.

264-265 According to tradition, the tall stem of the gondola symbolizes the curve of the Grand Canal, the six points at the front symbolize the six neighborhoods into which Venice is divided, and the one at the back symbolizes La Giudecca.

265 bottom The forcola (rowlock), which is fitted into a special housing on the gondola, is made of a single piece of walnut burr and finished like a veritable woodcarving.

According to legend, it incorporates the characteristic lightness of sea foam, raised up on the tail of a generous mermaid as a wedding present for a bridegroom who resisted her lures. You have to see for yourself the incredible motions of an elderly lacemaker in Burano to realize how seemingly clumsy old hands can move with truly unbelievable agility and unravel a complex web of what does indeed appear to be seaweed and sea foam. These older ladies are the only repositories of a complex body of knowledge, and they are capable of producing infinite variations, forming intricate patterns as they wish.

Mask-making was once so common that there was actually a mask-makers' guild in Venice. Masks were introduced into Venice after the conquest of the Levant, and soon they were all the rage, becoming an essential accessory even for the nobility. They were worn for almost 6 months of the year, at times fixed by the rigid Venetian ceremonial calendar, giving strangers to the city the impression of a delightful, endless carnival. The trade was recently revived to recreate the magic of carnival time. People put on a new face to forget, a new skin to rejuvenate themselves, a new screen of paper mâché to conceal their desires and weaknesses from prying. Venice is not the only city in Veneto with similar craft traditions. Ancient trades such as pottery making are also to be found on the mainland. At Bassano del

266 A full-scale industry has grown up to produce paper mâché masks with creative and grotesque shapes since the Venice Carnival was revived in 1980.

266-267 The craft of wood gilding is still carried on by some small cottage industries in Venice, especially in the construction and restoration of antique picture frames and small carvings.

267 top There are some great
masters of woodcarving in
Veneto, especially in the
mountains, but this craft is
no longer quite so genuine as
it once was, because its
practitioners mainly cater to
the tourist market.

267 bottom The resounding
forge of Vulcan has some
outstanding imitators in
Veneto, the home of the last
great masters of wrought
iron descended from the
Bellotto and Rizzarda
dynasties and also sculptor
Toni Benetton.

Grappa, in the magnificent setting of Palazzo Sturm, overlooking the River Brenta just a stone's throw from the famous bridge, visitors can see the development of this craft across the ages, from the magnificent eighteenth-century Manardi and Antonibon ceramics made at Nove di Bassano to recent contemporary creations designed by artists of international repute.

It is a pity that pottery is commonly known as a "poor man's art form," because the expression does not do justice to the wealth of imagination and creativity that adds quality and artistic beauty to this simple raw material.

The same applies to the mountain tradition of woodworking and woodcarving, both of which are very common in the Belluno area, where artists of the caliber of Augusto Murer of Falcade have numerous disciples. In the field of wrought iron Veneto has also produced masters of Art Nouveau like Umberto Bellotto of Venice and Carlo Rizzarda of Feltre and, more recently, Toni Benetton of Treviso, who have raised the blacksmith's trade to the level of an art. Wealth and luxury are the province of more noble materials like gold and silver, and the jewelers of present-day Vicenza could easily have amazed the noble ladies of ancient Versailles with their refined tastes.

269 left The art of producing decorative blown glass with colored pastes, aventurine, milk-scab, and murrine (tiny colored glass cylinders) has been perfected over the centuries in Murano, and a crucial contribution to the craft has been made by famous designers and some of the leading artists of the 20th century.

269 top right Burano is particularly famous for the type of needle lace known as punto in aria, in which only needle and thread are used, without any background fabric.

269 bottom right The art of ceramic making is widespread in the Vicenza area, and exhibitions are regularly held at the attractive Palazzo Sturm in Bassano to keep the tradition alive.

270-271 It's traditional to dress up at Carnival time in Venice, but the city's residents do so less and less often, because the city is invaded by tourists vying to outdo one another in their colorful costumes.

270 bottom and 271 bottom right Until the Venice Carnival was revived about 20 years ago to encourage tourism to return in what had been the low season, the tradition had remained dormant for centuries.

Veneto means tradition: true, sincere folk traditions, not just shows put on for the benefit of tourists like the Venice Carnival, which was revived in 1980 after an absence of nearly two centuries, much changed from its historical predecessor. Once, the Venetians wore attractive masks to conceal their identity, but nowadays, in the consumer society, those who wear masks and costumes do so merely to show off at a huge party held in the delightful showplace of Venice. To rediscover the healthy enthusiasm of long ago you have to look elsewhere, at events like the Regatta or the Vogalonga boat race, when traditional craft rowing down the meandering Grand Canal or through the quivering reaches of the lagoon can be admired in a more or less competitive spirit, or at the Chiesa del Redentore, under a hail of fireworks that illuminate the night as bright as day amid a swarm of bobbing boats. Every nose is turned skywards, and cries of joy or criticisms are uttered by the last real Venetians, now relegated to the role of extras in a city that has sold its soul to the tourists.

The joyful revelry of the ancient popular festivals is still to be found in Veneto in the rustic "bread and wine" festivals held on the eve of Epiphany around huge bonfires made from massive piles of wood and stubble to celebrate two of the most important products of the harvest. The direction taken by the sparks of the bonfire is interpreted as an auspicious sign or, much more rarely, as a warning of lean years to come. Over a glass of mulled wine and the auspicious songs of the occasion, the spirits take care not to disturb the atmosphere of merrymaking, because the old-fashioned Veneto recipe for good health and good cheer (rather more nourishing than

271 top left and top right One of the greatest amusements for tourists is to pose for hours in front of the most famous monuments in Venice, hoping that a famous cameraman will immortalize the most unusual costumes.

272 *The Wake of the Redeemer, held on the third Saturday in July, is one of the most popular festivals with Venetians. This ancient tradition derives from the celebrations held to mark the end of the terrible plague of 1576.*

272-273 The Lion of
St. Mark on the quay is
silhouetted against the sky,
while colorful fireworks are
set off from the rafts floating
on the Giudecca canal at the
traditional Redeemer festival.

273 bottom A firework
display held in St. Mark's
Basin is watched by the
whole population of Venice
with their traditional boats,
decorated for the occasion
with tree branches and
colored lamps.

274-275 *The Vogalonga regatta, inaugurated in 1975 to revive the "Veneto-style rowing" tradition, is now internationally famous.*

274 bottom left *One phase of the non-competitive Vogalonga regatta concludes when the crews row under the Three Arches bridge crossing the Cannaregio canal, cheered on by the crowd.*

274 bottom right and 275 bottom *The typical regatta boats are the gondola and the fast gondolino, followed by the caorlina, a lagoon cargo boat, the pupparino, named after the streamlined shape of the poop, the sandolo, a fishing and pleasure raft, and its close relative the mascareta.*

275 top and center *The Historic Regatta, which originated in the Middle Ages, although the present version only dates from 1899, is held in Venice on the first Sunday in September.*

"an apple a day keeps the doctor away") is still applicable today: "Wear your hat, eat chicken pills, drink wine, and send the doctors off to have a good time." The genuine carnival can be seen in Verona, where it retains its traditional spirit and there is an atmosphere of spontaneous collective gaiety, led by the "Father of Gnocchi," who actually receives his investiture in the Church of St. Zeno.

According to tradition, that neighborhood was the birthplace of the generous Tommaso da Vico, a benefactor who provided plenty of bread, flour, butter, wine, and cheese to make gnocchi for distribution to the hungry populace during the famine of 1530.

The "Father of Gnocchi," an extravagant character with a white or multi-colored suit and a bit of a belly, initiates the "Gnocchi Bacchanalia" on the last Friday before Lent, brandishing a huge fork with a gnocco stuck on it. There are also costume festivals with historical pageants, the best-known of which is held in conjunction with Venice's historic Regatta on the Grand Canal, when colorful eight-oared gondolas escort the gondola bearing the Doge and Caterina Cornaro, Queen of Cyprus and widow of Lusignano, who donated her precious kingdom to the Republic of Venice in 1489, receiving the delightful residence of Asolo in exchange.

Still in the province of Venice, the Noale pageant, held at the end of June, features flag tossers and musicians, and comes to a spectacular conclusion with the burning of the tower.

The Marciliana pageant, held in Chioggia during the third weekend of June, commemorates the victory won in 1380, when the people of Chioggia fought alongside the Venetians against the Genoese.

The pageant, founded quite recently, but based on detailed historical research, is named after a characteristic Chioggia boat and involves three contests: the archery contest, the scaule race (scaule are small boats manned by four oarsmen and two crossbowmen, normally used to escort noblemen or the mayor), and the crossbowmen's relay.

Other famous events are the Feltre pageant, already mentioned, and the equally celebrated pageant of the ten Montagnana towns, involving a horse race in which expert jockeys represent the 10 communities of the ancient Lombard district of Montagnana. The pageant has ancient origins: it commemorates the liberation of the towns from the tyranny of Ezzelino III da Romano.

The most famous of these enjoyable costume events is the living chess game played every two years (in even years) at Marostica on the second Sunday in September. Back in 1454, the city was ruled by Mayor Taddeo Parisio, a man of intellect and, some say, a humanist. Two proud noblemen, Vieri di Vallonara and Rinaldo di Angaran, both claimed the hand of Lionora, his daughter. Finding himself charged, yet again, with ruling on an affair of the heart, he decided to apply to the letter an ancient ordinance which required such questions to be resolved without bloodshed over the chessboard.

After a number of moves accompanied by a running commentary from the herald, the goddess of fortune, blind as love, eventually decided in favor of Lionora's favorite, Vieri di Vallonara.

However, his adversary was not left empty-handed. As a consolation prize for being check-mated, the mayor gave him the hand of his sister Oldrada, who was less attractive than her young niece. This civilized decision, which left the tricky question to be decided by human ability and intellectual qualities rather than the brute force of the rivals, can teach us something even now.

Now we have played our match, but do not know whether we have won or lost. The stakes were high, but those who defend the colors of Veneto begin with an advantage, and we will leave it up to the reader to judge the outcome.

278 top The streets of Chioggia are filled with period costumes and weapons on the third weekend in June, during the Marciliana pageant held to commemorate the victory of 1380 when Chioggia fought with Venice against Genoa.

278 bottom This photo shows the traditional costume worn by the women of Cortina d'Ampezzo at folk festivals.

278-279 A delightful chess game, held in the mediaeval setting of Marostica, commemorates the rivalry between two gentlemen for the hand of the beautiful madonna Lionora.

279 bottom The traditional carnival character from Sappada called Rollate is named after the jangling bronze balls tied around his waist which announce his arrival, brandishing a broom, to open the Carnival procession.

280-281 This traditional wooden effigy from the Sappada Carnival is supposed to release the ancient spirits of fertility so that they banish the rigors of winter and reawaken the spring as soon as possible.

282 *Standing at the main entrance of the Palazzo della Signoria is the best loved Florentine statue, Michelangelo's David. The original is conserved in the Accademia delle Belle Arti.*

284-285 *The Torre del Mangia, the Duomo, the Campanile, the red roofs of the palazzi: the prodigious splendor of Siena is captured in a single shot.*

286-287 *The church of Santa Maria della Spina lays on the banks of the Arno in Pisa. Threatened by periodic flooding, the church was demolished during the last century and then reconstructed.*

288-289 *The Ponte Vecchio in Florence is known throughout the world as the goldsmiths' bridge because of the craftsmen who have traded there since the time of Cosimo I.*

the horizons of art and beauty
TUSCANY

the horizons of art and beauty

TUSCANY

CONTENTS

291 Cypresses are one of the
characteristic elements of the
Sienese landscape. They line
the twisting roads and the
crests of the hills, delineate
the meadows and fields, and
often constitute the only tall
plants in the region.

INTRODUCTION

How difficult it is to write about Tuscany. One is swamped by the tritest of clichés to the point where it seems impossible to find even a single phrase that has not already been used by an art historian, a poet, a naturalist, an anthropologist, or an ordinary, casual visitor. There is a certain magnetism about Tuscany, and there must be very few people, Italian or otherwise, who have not at some point exclaimed "Oh, how I'd like to live in Florence!," or "how I'd love a cottage in the Chianti hills!" Mention the "Sienese countryside" and up pop idyllic images done to death by the advertising industry: long twisting roads cutting through bright green fields punctuated by vineyards and beautiful stone farmhouses, a pair of grazing horses or perhaps a village inhabited by cheerful farmers and fairy tale peasant girls, not to mention the greatest of Tuscany's friends, those foreigners for whom the Grand Tour has never gone out of fashion. Following in the footsteps of Byron, Dickens, Rogers, Wordsworth, and Forster, they return in perhaps less sophisticated, but decidedly more numerous and worldly groups. They overlook the myriad incongruities, the erratic museum opening hours, the pizzas served in front of the Palazzo della Signoria, the panini offered in Piazza del Campo and even the tacky, illuminated plastic reproductions of the Leaning Tower of Pisa.

They could hardly return to Hamburg, Minneapolis, or Osaka and say that yes, they wanted to take a look at Tuscany, but their time was up after Rome and Venice. For Italians, on the other hand, Tuscany is a rather distant "mamma," almost too beautiful and famous. She is not arrogant by any means, willing as she is to put herself on show and invite us to share in her riches, but nevertheless well aware of her position. In contrast with Rome, torn between her imperial glory and the trattorie of the Trastevere, between ministerial limousines and Cinecittà, between nobility and "the people," and in contrast with Venice where the tourist industry has succeeded in destroying the magic, Florence has preserved its essentially provincial character. Ready to welcome, it is just as quick to close in on itself and be content with its glorious past, its brief tenure as capital under the Savoias, and even more content to have returned to its role as Queen of that most peaceful, photographed, painted, and described of lands. With its crown of art cities and less obvious, but nonetheless brilliant, minor gems with its harsh, rocky islands and generous but occasionally treacherous mountains, and with that musical language with its beautifully judged accents and tones Tuscany is enchanting.

Although Italian was created here, the Tuscans speak a language of their own, the full range of which no imitator could ever hope to reproduce. It is the language of a deep-rooted culture, one so charming as to grace each and every one of the region's inhabitants, making them all, if only for an instant, Dante's favorite grandson.

293 Massive and soaring, forming part of a monumental complex of extraordinary power, Santa Maria del Fiore is, with its Brunelleschi dome and the Baptistery, the spiritual center of the city.

294-295 The Uccellina Mountains constitute two thirds of the Maremma Natural Park, a wild unspoiled oasis, a maze of trees and shrubs in which the only signs of man's passing are the ruins of the watchtowers.

296-297 Pitigliano, in the Maremma, high on an outcrop of tuff, has Etruscan origins but was at its peak in the Middle Ages as a fief of the Aldobrandeschi and the Orsini.

298-299 Fluttering in the wind is the symbol of the Goose, one of the seventeen neighborhoods in the town of Siena that compete, in July and August, with feverish intensity for victory in the Palio, a traditional centuries-old horse race.

THE STONES
OF HISTORY

300 and 301 The Florentine monuments form part of our collective consciousness. Palazzo Vecchio, Brunelleschi's dome, and Giotto's Tower are part of humanity's patrimony, visited by millions of tourists but still capable of arousing profound emotion.

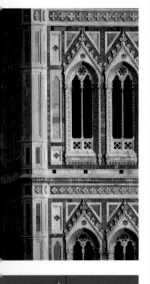

At the turn of the century the young Lucy Honeychurch, armed with her faithful Baedeker guide, arrived in Florence with very clear intentions: to take a room with a view at the Pensione Bertolini, experience Italian art at first hand and, if at all

What kind of an adventure she did not know. What she did know is that only in Florence could her thirst for life and beauty be satisfied. Lucy was following in the footsteps of thousands of Britons, Germans, and Americans, all traveling on the Grand Tour, the indispensable finishing touch to the education of any well-bred young person of the era. Arriving in Tuscany in those times must have been very different. The search for decent accommodation, a reliable driver, and a restaurant themselves constituted an adventure. But have things changed so very much since then? No, not really. Tuscany and its art cities, large and small, are still essential sights. Adventures are still there to be experienced by those with a spirit open to beauty, harmony, genius, and the unusual. And, all things considered, the search for a good hotel is still something of a gamble. The grand tours are still arriving from Britain, Germany, and America, and now also from Japan and the rest of the world. Today, they are brisker, more worldly, and occasionally (but not always) better organized.

The first stop is always Florence: perhaps out of respect, perhaps for the sake of convenience.

The trains drawing into Santa Maria Novella station and the buses parked in Piazzale Michelangelo daily disgorge thousands of tourists eager to devour Florentine Madonnas and Della Robbia babies. They put up with the indescribable humidity of the summer, the interminable treks, and the lines at the entrances to museums. How could one return to Bonn or Osaka and admit to not having seen the Tondo Doni, or not to have gasped at the climb to the top of the Campanile, Giotto's Tower? The tour is completed with the aid of a variety of history of art guides and novels, risking to overload the intellect at the expense of the heart and imagination.

Weighed down with the writings of Ruskin, Browning, Stendahl, and Goethe, it hard to believe that this is a living city, and not a miraculous relic of the Middle Ages and the Renaissance. Florence is of course a city that relies heavily on tourism, but it

manages to treat it as something that has fallen into its lap by chance. So much so that the last visitors to be received with authentic joy and relief were the youngsters armed with sleeping bags who arrived in that tragic November of 1966 to save Florence's masterpieces from the fury of the flooding Arno. Far from allowing themselves to be overwhelmed, the Florentines regard the "three-day trippers" with a hint of derisive insolence. It is in fact perhaps true to say that for the modern Florentines, historic Florence is more of a burden than a source of revenue and international fame, like an inheritance that is difficult to run and to administrate. As early as the 1950's that acute observer Mary MacCarthy wrote: "History, for Florence, is neither legend nor eternity, but a massive weight of rough building stone demanding continual repairs, pressing on the modern city like a debt, blocking progress."However, if the Florentines of the past had decided that progress was not for them, what language would be spoken in Italy today? What masterpieces would people be able to admire in the museums and galleries? What would be the state of political and social developments on the peninsula? While not wishing to load the descendants of Dante, Giotto, and Machiavelli with too much responsibility, it is nonetheless true to say that nothing is further removed from the Florentine spirit than the concept that art, beauty, and great ideas are the fruit of a sacred respect for tradition. Florence, the offspring of Rome in the Middle Ages, a second Athens during the Renaissance, has always shied away from mere supporting roles inventing, century after century, its own identity and exporting it with pride. One of the characteristics most typically Florentine is that of looking beyond one's own horizons. The "castrum" founded by Fiorinus, one of Julius Caesar's generals, guarded the consular roads leading to Rome, Lucca, Pisa, and Faenza. This laid the basis for future trade and diplomatic missions. Their journeying led the Florentines to accept and export ideas and products, while still maintaining a precise identity and a desire to return to their homeland. Above all they demonstrated a subtle and at times insidious insolence towards the established order, with a distinct preference for argument and brawling, or at least for a cruel joke.

This is what history, stories, and literature have taught us and from the clashes with the other Tuscan cities and from the perpetual struggles between the rival factions. Nor did Florence ever suffer from a sense of inferiority to Rome, the cradle of civilization.

The proclamation by which in 1296 Arnolfo di Cambio was entrusted with the construction of the Duomo as a replacement for the old church of Santa Reparata was clear in its intentions. Florence wanted a building capable of exceeding in dimensions and magnificence anything that had been created in the golden ages of Rome and Greece. Anything more explicit is hard to imagine.

Although the resulting building cannot match the majesty of the Parthenon, the beauty of Santa Maria del Fiore is breathtaking, thanks in part to the additions by Giotto and Brunelleschi. A cardinal point and the ideal beginning to any tour, the duomo can even be seen from the highway, an apparition which forms part of the collective consciousness not only of the Italians but of the entire world. It is a cardinal point of the city, but by no means its only attraction. Those intent on visiting the whole of Florence should dedicate more than the three days of the typical all-inclusive tour. The museums alone number around sixty. Each church is a museum in itself. And, there are the palazzi, the bridges, and the picturesque streets. So much for Baedeker!

One risks an overdose of art, a full-blown case of Stendahl's Syndrome. Florence could be just too much for visitor with refined and broad-based, but not inexhaustible interests. No lesser personage than Henry James, who was certainly no inexperienced loafer, had to admit to being a little overwhelmed.

A glance at a map of the Florentine monuments is enough to give one an idea of the challenge involved. Taking into account just the historic triangle formed by the Fortezza da Basso, San Marco Square, and the Forte di Belvedere, excluding therefore Fiesole, San Miniato, Le Cascine Park, and the more modest quarters, there is not a single street, turn, or piazza which fails to provide at least one feature worthy of note. However, this in a city which could never have been accused of wanting to turn itself into a permanent museum. Even though

the mass of tourists has stimulated the proliferation of bars and fast food joints, souvenir stands, and crib-guides with their "must see" lists, Florence remains a place in which people live, work, and enjoy activities other than the "systematic skimming" practiced by the tourists. This is a characteristic which is thankfully shared by all the great Tuscan cities of art.

If one follows the course of the Arno almost to its mouth, as far as Pisa, a great, historic and unfortunate rival to Florence, one finds something of the same spirit. Although the Pisans boast wonders which people throughout the world can recognize, they themselves have above all been great travelers, traders, and academics.

Pisa was also situated on the routes of two great consular roads, the Aurelia and the Emilia Scauria, which linked it with Rome, Provence, and as far off as the Baltic. But first and foremost it had one of the two ports fundamental to traffic on the Mediterranean: a source of great wealth, not only in financial terms. The monumental complex of the Campo dei Miracoli with the Duomo, the Campanile, the Baptistery, and the Camposanto would itself be sufficient to ensure Pisa's eternal glory.

The image of the Leaning Tower is in all probability one of the ten most famous in the world. It is a universal symbol, albeit one devalued by the countless plastic reproductions which transform it into ash-trays, paper weights, clocks, and tacky ornaments, and make of it a classic example of tourist kitsch. An idealized link between heaven and Earth, the Tower was erected in a seafarers' town. Nowadays, the Tyrrhenian Sea seems a long way off, separated by a 6 mile stretch of river. And yet Pisa still retains a vague saltiness in the air. This very salt is responsible for the corrosion of the marble on the facades of the churches.

The smell of the sea blends with that of the river which here, in contrast to Florence where it rushes past, appears resigned to its impending fate. Everything is more relaxed, although history has not spared Pisa its dramatic moments of great political success and severe defeat. The years between 1000 and 1300 witnessed prodigious development both in the city itself and in the surrouding region.

302 Diosalvi conceived the Baptistery at Pisa as a grandiose circular temple, with the exterior imaginatively subdivided into three increasingly light orders: blind arcades on columns and arched loggias perforated like fine lace.

303 The foundation of the Tower dates back to 1173 and is attributed to Bonanno. The design called for a much higher tower than the current one (circa 180 feet) but subsidence, cause of the famous lean, forced the adoption of a more modest structure.

304-305 *The unusual form of the Campanile of the Duomo at Pistoia (above, a detail) is the result of the vicissitudes that have marked its history. It was first a Lombard tower, then the civic tower, and only took on its present form in the sixteenth century.*

Having become a great maritime power, Pisa celebrated its triumphs with a series of illustrious monuments, and saw its population rise to the notable total of 40,000 inhabitants. It was only following the defeat against Meloria that decadence set in through wars, the loss of its independence, shortages, floods, and epidemics.

A sequence of tragedies which would have brought any civilization to its knees. At least in Pisa, now isolated inland, the memories of its greatness remain. Apart from the Campo dei Miracoli (a bizarre name, given that in the Middles Ages the piazzas so called were the theaters of charlatans and tumblers), the list is impressive. There are numerous churches, palazzi, piazzas, and wonders like Santa Maria della Spina, a pale and minuscule Gothic jewel, a triumph of spires and stone carving, which in the second half of the nineteenth century was completely demolished and reconstructed in identical form a few yards further back to save it from continual flooding.

Pinnacles and steeples are often found in Pisan architecture as a kind of indelible symbol, a perpetual memorial to an all too brief and intense golden age. The bitterness of defeat was attenuated to some extent by the fame, even abroad, of the city's university. The Pisan institute, "Lo Studio," was the first to be given official recognition with the Papal bull "In Supremae dignitatis" from Clement VI in 1343.

The tradition of Pisa as a seat of learning continued and with the "Scuola Normale," founded by Napoleon in 1810, the city was again at the forefront of higher education. The tradition had far reaching roots. Apart from the oft-cited Galileo Galilei and his experiments into the isochronicity of the pendulum in the Duomo, Pisa is linked with a veritable legend of the world of mathematics, Leonardo Fibonacci. Fibonacci identified a series of numbers of very precise proportions (each being the sum of the two preceding figures) which could be found in countless natural phenomena. It is hard to say whether anything of his geniality still remains in the city, but what is certain is that one of its current assets is represented by its students, who arrive not only from all over Italy, but also from abroad. Thus, for thousands of years, Pisa has remained a young, broad-minded city.

304 bottom The Baptistery of Pistoia, built between 1338 and 1359, according to plans by Andrea Pisano, is an elegant Gothic structure with an octagonal base, and covered with white and green marble. In this picture, one can see the upper section of one of the three portals, all of which are decorated with finely worked statues, reliefs in white marble, and geometric decorative motifs.

305 top The Duomo at Pistoia, characterized by an elegant colonnade with glazed terracotta vaults by Andrea Della Robbia, was begun in the fifth century and rebuilt with significant modifications in the thirteenth century.

305 bottom Giovanni Pisano left two works of extraordinary emotive and artistic impact in the church of Sant'Andrea at Pistoia: a wooden crucifix and, above all, the pulpit with deep relief carvings illustrating the story of the redemption.

Pisa retains a cosmopolitan tradition which led a scandalized prelate in the times of Matilde di Canossa to declare: "The city is contaminated by pagans, Turks, Libyans, Parthians, and dark-skinned Chaldeans wandering the beaches." Clearly, racial and religious contamination was not frowned upon by the Pisans, but rather treated with indulgence. A great influx of foreigners meant great mercantile and maritime success. The wider the horizons, the richer the harvest of ideas. Today the tourists remain alongside the students, but are however excluded from the lives of the permanent guests. The Pisans, like the Florentines, maintain a detached distance between themselves and those who believe that they can get to know their city in just a few hours. Less forthcoming and more discreet, the Pisans only ever let themselves go on particular occasions such as the "Gioco del Ponte," once decidedly violent but now somewhat tamer. At these times the combative spirit of eight centuries ago when the struggles were against Amalfi, Genoa, and Venice, reappears and the Pisan character gets heated. There is an international air at Siena too, despite the rather paradoxical fact that this is perhaps one of the most tenaciously provincial Tuscan cities. In the case of Siena this is by no means a pejorative term, but rather an affectionate description of a civic life-style that has somehow survived, at least in part, the delusions of history. Isolated, and of an almost absolute medieval purity, it has often been asked

306 top The cathedral at Arezzo enjoys a magnificent setting and is approached by a flight of steps. The theme is continued inside with frescoes and large stained-glass windows and culminates in Piero della Francesca's Magdalen.

what it is about Siena that has, for motives that occasionally appear unjust, prevented modernity from making any more than minor incursions within its walls. And, above all, it is asked why, at a particular historical moment, in this particular place, blessed by a series of fortunate circumstances, a school of painting was created which boasts at least four names fundamental to the history of art: Duccio di Buoninsegna, Simone Martini, and the two Lorenzettis.

306 bottom The earliest surviving work by Cimabue, the Crucifix, is conserved in the church of San Domenico. The bright colors and the pain-wracked face inspire a profoundly emotional religious charge.

307 The thirteenth century church of San Francesco is a veritable gallery of art. In the choir the remarkable fresco cycle by Piero della Francesca dedicated to the Legend of the True Cross provides a resumé of the themes of renaissance painting.

This phenomenon rocked the art world from the thirteenth century to the Renaissance, and can perhaps be explained by the character of the Sienese themselves. The adjectives which have, over the centuries, been applied to them are countless and often contradictory: bizarre, versatile, chivalrous, sentimental, free, heroic, gay, and dramatic.

The Florentines, who never got on with the Sienese, said with a touch of malice that their character was inherited not from the Romans, who are considered to have founded the city, but from the Gauls led by Brenno, or the uncivilized Germanic barbarians. Whatever its origins, the Sienese character is one of intense collective pride, the best expression of which is to be found in the "Palio delle Contrade." It is also revealed in art that lavishly indulges in gold and color, with energy, mystic ecstasy, and proud celebration of civic glories, demonstrated in the Good Government cycle by Ambrogio Lorenzetti. In Siena art has always been a public triumph. Duccio di Buoninsegna's last brush stroke on the Maestà was the signal for three days of collective celebrations. Today it still seems that the detachment of man's artistic creations from the lives of the city's inhabitants is less accentuated at Siena than elsewhere. Perhaps the merit is due to its compact dimensions and essentially medieval layout.

Siena, like a well-fed snail, fills every nook and cranny of its shell, it turns away cars, invites visitors to walk and climb the steps of San Giovanni, and to wander with the wafting scent of the spices used to flavor the "panforte."

Coming in from the country, the yellow-ochre Crete and the green hills, the terracotta red of the buildings, the campanili, and the slim Gothic shapes seem perfectly integrated, almost spontaneous outcrops of the land. In fact, city and country exist in a symbiotic relationship at Siena, and one senses that below the herring-bone pattern cobbles of the Campo the city's three hills converge. One also senses that the shell-like form was not the result of some planner's whim, but rather derives from a precise geomorphologic structure. There is little sense in discussing Siena and only mentioning Piazza del Campo in passing, and not only because Montaigne rightly (with all due apologies to the Venetians)

defined it as the world's most beautiful piazza. What is more important is that Piazza del Campo is a concentration of Siena's civic history, often combined with elements of its religious history which finds its focus higher up in the massive bulk of the Duomo. The market was held in the Campo. In the past as it still does today, water arrived in the Campo to feed the Fonte Gaia via a 16 mile long aqueduct. But above all, the Campo was the area for those games for which the Sienese went literally crazy. The Palio was of course the most famous, but there were also more bloody and fanciful contests which reflected, in a sporting light, those which took place outside the city walls against enemies rather less inclined to fight. The oldest and perhaps the most bizarre was that of the "pugna," a form of boxing, the aim of which was simply to beat the living daylights out of one's opponent. Then there was the "Mazzascudo" game in which contestants with wicker baskets on their heads beat one another with the active participation of the spectators. Mortal injuries were no more than unfortunate consequences of the game.

"Panem et Circenses," as the Roman ancestors had taught, holds true in Siena. The Sienese passion for sports has always been so intense that, as legend has it, it was they who taught the Spanish, long-term dominators, the rules and customs of bullfighting. It is a city always ready for a joke and demonstrating intense passion, but also capable of heart-stopping delicacy. Siena is irresistible at dusk on a summer's evening, as the sun slowly sinks behind the towers and roofs tinting the terracotta an even deeper shade of red. It is this curious blend of violence and harmony, rage and affection, which makes Siena a city of exquisite memories for all.

The three Tuscan "capitals," Florence, Pisa, and Siena, are flanked by a court of regal princesses. Lucca, Arezzo, and Pistoia, and also Grosseto, Livorno (Leghorn), Massa, and Carrara, are often overlooked in the lists of the great cities of art. Lucca certainly merits the closest of attention, not least because it represents the last resting place of the beautiful, beloved Ilaria del Caretto, wife of Paolo di Guinigi, nobleman of the city. Her tomb has won the hearts of generations of romantics, but unfortunately

309 top left Little of the original Sienese style is left in the Duomo at Grosseto. The facade was completely rebuilt in the first half of the nineteenth century. While the interior has also lost its original structure, you can still admire an attractive font and altar dedicated to the Madonna delle Grazie by Antonio Ghini.

309 top right Grosseto, the Cinderella of Tuscan cities, has hidden surprises for those who look further than the imposing walls which enclose the oldest part of the town, and which in the nineteenth century were converted to a public walkway.

309 bottom In the ancient heart of the city, enclosed by the walls, extends Piazza Dante, once known as the Cisternone or the Piazza of the Chains. The city is relatively young, being founded after the year 935 when the ancient Roselle was devastated by the Saracens and was definitively abandoned in favor of the small castle of Grosseto.

has also attracted the attentions of vandals armed with pencils and, more recently, felt-tip pens. Jacopo della Quercia, sculptor and in this case exceptional portraitist, captured all her composed grace and serene beauty. These could also be the adjectives most suited to Lucca, a tranquil elderly lady, protected by imposing and seemingly impregnable city walls. Behind its turrets the city has changed very little, preserving a character which falls somewhere between the noble and the affable, a somewhat neglected minor capital. The best loved street is undoubtedly Via Filungo, civilly (and also inevitably given its dimensions) reserved for pedestrians. The street could justifiably be compared with the Mercerie in Venice, but which in spite of the opulence of its shop windows, also has something in common with an eastern souk. It is incredible to think that over a century ago Lucca risked seeing its structure obliterated: in 1866 the city walls were put up for sale, on offer to private building speculators. They were bought by the town council and there were plans in the air for some time to demolish them to make way for some unknown project. Fortunately the citizens protested, thus saving one of the most suggestive walks in Tuscany. Provincial enough to make it a haven for numerous exhausted city-dwellers, a stone's throw from some sublime countryside and punctuated by extraordinary villas, Lucca is and always has been a wealthy town of traders and bankers. The height of its economic, political, and artistic power came in the thirteenth century, when the Lucchese began to acquire a reputation for being astute and intelligent merchants. Well aware of their inability to compete with Florence in fields such as wool, they specialized in silk. Their damasks, velvets, and gold and silver brocades were famous throughout the medieval world, enjoying success in France, Flanders, and England. The Lucchese exported textiles, but also citizens. Numerous important Lucchese families were to be found in Paris, Montpellier, and the Champagne region, and they played a vital role in improving relationships between the European potentates.

This was of course the period of greatest artistic splendor in the town. The Romanesque style of Lucca is a blend of solidity, simplicity, and a desire for

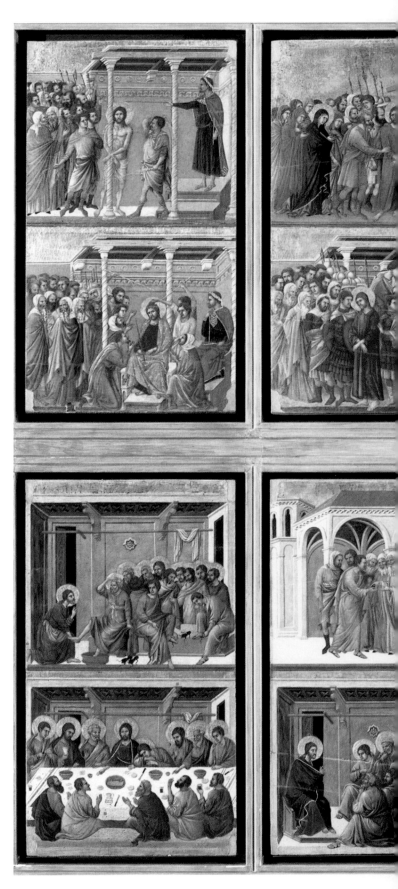

310-311 The completion of Duccio da Buoninsegna's Maestà (the illustration shows a detail of the reverse side of the panel), today kept in Siena's Museo dell'Opera Metropolitana, was the starting point for three days of festivities involving the entire city. A masterpiece of Sienese painting from the sixteenth century, the Maestà is a complex and fascinating creation and soon became a model for other compositions on the same theme.

clarity. Only later did the influence of Pisa introduce more extravagant forms.

This was also the beginning of a love-hate relationship with Florence. Allies when it suited both parties, but more frequently enemies, Lucca was destined to submit, to turn in on itself, and to concentrate on defending its very existence, improving civic life and increasing trade.

However, conflicts and conspiracies were not lacking at Lucca either, such as the celebrated case of the "Burlamacchi." It is as if to say that when foreign policy is disappointing, there is always internal strife to fall back on. Were it not so, how could one bear such perfect peace in which strolling a couple of miles outside the city walls plunges one into the paradise of Lucca's surrounding countryside. The outlying villas merit a chapter to themselves. Like the Venetian villas of the Riviera del Brenta, they represent the wealth, good taste, and desire for entertainment of the good citizens who, exhausted by the cares of business, had monumental masterpieces erected for their vacations. The most celebrated examples are Villa Mansi at Segromigno, dating back to the sixteenth century but rebuilt two centuries later by Juvara, Villa della Gattaiola, Villa Orsetti, and Villa Torrigiani.

Equally tied to the land and the countryside, Pistoia is a town which has experienced few moments of grandeur and numerous episodes of defeat. The anonymous chronicler of the "Istorie Pistoiesi" writes of dark times in which conflicts and sectarian strife transformed the town and its countryside into a theater of massacres until 1306 when it fell to the Florentines. At that point the massacre extended to the works of art, and as the spirit of revenge died forever, it left in its place a sober melancholy. The conquerors destroyed all evidence of the former power, demolishing the towers and the city walls.

The Pistoiese tried to resist, but with little success, and early in the fifteenth century they became in practice the subjects of the neighboring city. Perhaps this is why among all the Tuscans they are the least concerned with celebrating their past.

They prefer to forget. The "Giostra dell'Orso," revived following the Second World War after centuries of neglect, has no precise historical references.

Here they prefer to treat the Duomo, the beautiful Romanesque, churches and the compact medieval nucleus as integral parts of civic life, rather than as treasures there to be fawned over. Yet the art of Pistoia is by no means second rate. Beginning with the works left by Coppo di Marcovaldo, now recognized as the teacher of Cimabue, one can admire a great crucifix in the Duomo. In the fourteenth century Giotto had a powerful influence on artists even out here in "provincial" Pistoia. Then there is the Romanesque architecture, the Gothic style of the Baptistery, and the church of San Paolo. But Pistoia is above all

a town of sculpture. In particular, the pulpit by Giovanni Pisano in the church of Sant'Andrea is an eternal symbol of recognition and devotion to the city that had taken in the artist. It is a work in which, as Pietro Toesca writes, "form is given to that 'visible speech' which Dante cherished in sculpture. No constriction tied the hand of the sculptor, even in the brief spaces afforded by the pendentives of the arches, in imagining those figures in acts which create complex harmonies, which collide with one another in a physical and spiritual agitation so intense as to refute comparison with any other masterpiece of Gothic art. The torments of the inner life appear to be the only factors determining the composition and form of each group and each figure, not through outward stylistic conventions, but through the expression of movement and passion." A long citation for a work composed only a little before the city's defeat, and which perhaps sums up the contradictory nature and spirit of the Pistoiese, destined to live unwillingly in the shadow of Florence. The last stop on our imaginary tour of metropolitan Tuscany is Arezzo, which Giorgio Saviane has defined as "concentrated Tuscany": from the limpid, petrified purity of the art of Piero

313 The original of Michelangelo's David is housed in the Galleria dell'Accademia in Florence where it is protected not only from the pollution in the Piazza della Signoria which threatened to ruin it, but also from attacks by vandals similar to the affront it suffered at the hand of a madman in 1991.

della Francesca to the immortal salacity of the "damned" writings of Pietro Aretino. Unfortunately modern town planning has eroded a great deal of the appeal commented on by the travelers of some decades ago. The changes have also affected the town's economic structure, with the arrival of important industries such as those of gold and clothing.

The changes do not, however, obscure the noble origins of the city. Arretium was one of the most important Etruscan cities, home of one of the twelve "lucumonie."

Wealthy and in a privileged position for trade, at the head of the three valleys of the Arno, the Tevere, and the Chiana, Arezzo had all the right credentials to become a center of fundamental importance.

This promise was fulfilled during the period of Roman domination, and was conserved through to the Middle Ages when civic life became more intense, in the shadow of the Lombards and the Marchesi of Tuscany, with the foundation of a law and literature school, closed in 1300. But like all Tuscan cities Arezzo is above all a city of art.

And the personification of the city is Piero della Francesca with his rigorous perspective, classical monumentality, and the Legend of the True Cross, the cycle of frescoes in the choir of the church of San Francesco. It is enough to look at a detail, the view of Arezzo, and to compare it with the mosaic of the city roofs to understand the degree to which the artist was in tune with the commission, and above all how he brought to it his own idea of crystalline clarity. The Legend is a work of maturity. The medieval stories of Jacopo da Varagine become episodes of the Renaissance, solemn exaltations of the concrete and the human, a sober and discreet nobility which is also a feature of the city's streets. Unfortunately the beauty of the ancient town center was disrupted during the last world war by tragic destruction, often compounded by examples of ill-judged building developments. The monumental zone has survived isolated and vainly protected by the sixteenth century fortress. Below the fortress, in Piazza Grande, the "Giostra del Saracino" is held in late summer and is, together with Siena's "Palio" and the Florentine "Historical Calcio," the most popular of the region's colorful traditional festivals.

314-315 *The Sleeping Child is one of the most famous works by Giovanni Duprè, a nineteenth century Sienese sculptor, follower of Canova, and champion of the neoclassical style. In his autobiographical writings Duprè described in a clear, lively style, the Tuscan artistic milieu of his era.*

315

FLORENCE,
OF ARMS
AND BEAUTY

316 The campanile of Santo Spirito, in the foreground, announces the panorama of roofs, domes, and towers which makes the aerial view of Florence an ambassador for Italian life and culture throughout the world.

316-317 Before it became the "realm" of the goldsmiths, the Ponte Vecchio was the meat market. The butchers were evicted definitively at the end of the sixteenth century with the charge of having besmirched the beauty of the site with the by-products of their trade.

319 *Civic might is expressed in the great religious and secular buildings. In the shadow of the duomo and the Palazzo Vecchio the city prospered, struggled, and became the capital of art.*

320-321 The Arno has
played a precise role in
history of Florence, and thus
in the changes which led to it
becoming a great center of
art. It was in fact the Arno
which supplied water to the
wool and leather industries
from which the wealth of the
medieval city was
accumulated and which
financed works of art.

320 bottom The Giardini di Bóboli, behind the magnificent Palazzo Pitti, were the work of Tribolo and Buontalenti. They represent one of the most felicitous examples of the Italianate garden.

321 top the Baptistery of the Duomo, dedicated to San Giovanni, has been perhaps one of the best loved Florentine monuments ever since the times of Dante.

321 bottom The bridges spanning the Arno have not enjoyed an easy life, battling against the fury of floods as well as human perfidy. During the Second World War they were all mined with the exception of the Ponte Vecchio.

322 and 323 "In Santa Croce with no Baedeker" is the title of a chapter in Forster's A Room With A View. Without a guide it is by no means easy to find one's way around the works of art which transform the austere church into an extraordinary gallery, the funeral monuments which inspired Foscolo, and the chapels containing masterpieces such as Donatello's Crucifix.

324-325 and 325 Just a few
steps away from the railroad
station, Santa Maria
Novella, one of the most
famous churches in Florence,
offers a remarkable sampling
of Gothic architecture. Work
on its construction began in
1249, plans were drawn up,
and construction was
directed by an architect from
the Dominican order of
monks until the work was

completed in 1360.
The facade of the church
constitutes a true indication
of the skills of the master
decorators. Even Leon
Battista Alberti worked on
the church. He designed the
portal, which was completed
between 1456 and 1470, and
all of the material that stands
above the handsome central
cornice, including the two
delicate lateral volutes.

326 It was Cosimo I who, in the second half of the sixteenth century, commissioned Giorgio Vassari to design the Palazzo degli Uffizi destined, as the name suggests, to house the judiciary and administrative offices. The building today holds the State Archives and, above all, the Galleria, probably one of the most famous and most visited art galleries in the world.

327 There are several dozen museums in Florence. The Museo di San Marco (top, left) is housed in the splendid convent where Fra' Angelico left a good number of his works. In the galleries of the Palazzo Vecchio (top, right) the Medici era can be relived, while the Galleria dell'Accademia (bottom) is visited above all for its great Michelangelo masterpieces such as the dramatic Pietà da Palestrina.

328 As in many other works by Leonardo da Vinci, the landscape in the background of the Annunciation was based on a reality as seen and transformed by the eye of a genius.

329 In the age of Dante, Cimabue, the author of the superb Madonna in Maestà, (now in the Galleria degli Uffizi), was considered to be a proud, arrogant, and self-important man. However, his works have an extraordinary expressive force with an agitated rhythm that relaxes in the faces of his saints.

330 and 331 For a long time Sandro Botticelli was considered to be a prophet of beauty. But with the Birth of Venus and Primavera he renders his conceptions in a symbolic, problematical painting linked to the neo-Platonic culture. Thus, his naked Venus is a symbol of the simplicity and purity of nature and faith, while Primavera removes itself from reality in order to go beyond it and enter into the complex world of allegory.

332 and 333 The Tondo Doni (conserved in the Uffizi) and the Pietà (in the Museo dell'Opera del Duomo) represent two fundamental moments in the career of Michelangelo Buonarroti. The Tondo is an early work based on the play of light with mellow tones. It has recently been returned to its original splendor after being seriously damaged in the 1993 explosion which devastated part of the Galleria. The Pietà, executed in the artist's prime, demonstrates his movement away from the formal sculptural models of ancient art towards a more personal and searching form of expression.

334-335 *Palazzo Medici-Riccardi, built by Michelozzo in the mid-fifteenth century, was the home of Cosimo il Vecchio, Lorenzo il Magnifico, Charles VIII of France, and Charles V of Spain. Imposingly elegant, the house was the renaissance prototype of the noble residence.*

335 *The Cappella de'Pazzi, in one of the cloisters of Santa Croce, was one of the last works by Filippo Brunelleschi. The artist was by then a master of his art and the formal perfection is rigorous, severe, and articulated by chromatic contrasts.*

336 *Piazza Santissima Annunziata, the most harmonious square in Florence, features two elegant baroque fountains completed by Pietro Tacca in 1629. This pictures shows a detail.*

337 *In Florence no one calls the Neptune Fountain by Bartolomeo Ammannati by its proper name. The Biancone as it became known failed to arouse much enthusiasm among the citizens, and in fact an irreverent rhyming verse was soon coined which ran "Oh Ammannato, oh Ammannato, what beautiful marble you've ruined."*

338-339 The most famous piece of Florentine sculpture, the David in Piazza della Signoria, was Michelangelo's vision of a beautiful, taut, and physically perfect youth, created by the sculptor at the height of his power.

340-341 Time has not been gentle with the Ponte Vecchio. Originally it was a wooden construction which was destroyed by a flood in 1333. In the middle of that same century, Neri di Fioravante erected the stone bridge which was damaged

by the retreating Germans at the end of the Second World War and then in the floods of 1966. Today it is one of Florence's best loved symbols, dutifully crossed by same tourists on the look out for bargains in the myriad jewellers' shops.

SIENA, THE EFFECT OF GOOD GOVERNMENT

342-343 and 343
From above, one can better appreciate the incredible urbanistic homogeneity that distinguishes Siena. The color red can be found in the pavement of the Campo, Siena's remarkable shell-shaped central square, in the roofs of the houses, and in the bricks of the ancient, battlemented palazzi, among them the exquisite Palazzo Sansedoni,

built in the years around the end of the thirteenth century and the beginning of the fourteenth. Nobles and commoners have always enjoyed the same rich scene of beauty, the same fine materials, and the same handsome unity of thought and purpose: to preserve their city's square as one of the world's most renowned abodes of the spirit.

344 and 344-345 It is here, between Piazza del Campo and the Duomo, that the public part of the Palio delle Contrade takes place. And the Sienese, in spite of their fiercely proud attachment to the quarter in which they were born, recognize the fundamental role played by both the symbolic monuments in the urban and social fabric of the city.

347 The story behind the building of the Duomo was long and complex and culminated in a unbuilt design for a grandiose extension which would have made the existing building the transept of the new cathedral. The work as it appears today is a synthesis of diverse designs including that of Giovanni Pisano, the author of many of the statues gracing the facade.

346 top left A reminder of the city's Roman origins, the Sienese wolf with the two twins sits on the top of a column in Piazza del Duomo.

346 bottom left The majority of the statues executed by Giovanni Pisano for the facade of the Duomo are now kept in the Museo dell'Opera Metropolitana to counter the ravages of time. However, the lyricism and vivacity of the artist remain intact, together with an intensely dramatic religiosity.

346 right The Campanile of the Duomo of Siena, constructed in 1313 to the design of Agostino di Giovanni and Agnolo di Ventura, features multi-colored marble decoration echoing the hues of the cathedral body.

348

348-349 The mosaics, executed by the Venetian Castellani in the second half of the nineteenth century, are similar to those of the Duomo at Orvieto and represent episodes in the life of the Virgin Mary, culminating in the Coronation.

349 The opulent facade of the Duomo, animated and graceful in spite of the weight of the central rose window, was begun by Giovanni Pisano at the end of the thirteenth century and completed by Giovanni di Cecco after 1376, drawing inspiration from the Duomo of Orvieto.

350 left The starry sky, the gilded angels, frescoes, stucco, and multi-colored marble: decorative riches are concentrated on the magnificent ceiling of the cathedral.

350 top right This enchanting picture of the interior of the Duomo, or Cathedral, emphasizes once again its grandeur and mass, highlighted by the faint daylight that envelops the exquisite mosaics.

350 bottom right The pulpit by Nicola Pisano and his collaborators was sculpted between 1266 and 1268. The narrative structure is rich and lively, characterized by great dynamism and drama of a decidedly Gothic nature. Statuary and architecture combine in an immensely expressive work.

351 The interior of the cathedral with its forest of pillars creating fantastic perspectives can at first sight leave one dazed and confused. The bands of black and white marble, the gold, the plethora of decorations and paintings, and the intricate pavement overwhelm the structure of the building while providing visitors with a concentrated summary of medieval art.

352 In his Maestà, conserved
in the Palazzo Pubblico in
Siena, Simone Martini
revisited the theme and
composition tackled
by Duccio di Buoninsegna,
adding a touch of humanity
and a more mobile, rarefied
light to the stately perfection
of the maestro.

352-353 *Duccio di Buoninsegna painted the monumental Maestà (now in the Museo dell'Opera del Duomo) for the high altar of the Duomo at Siena. This large composition* *represents the most grandiose work on wood panel of the Middle Ages. Its choral sacredness, freshness, and spirituality made it a fundamental model for the artists of the era.*

354-355 Of Siena's Palazzo Pubblico, it has been said that it synthesizes the architecture of all the fourteenth century palazzi of the city which, in one way or another, all owe a debt to its example. It forms a perfect backdrop to the Campo, one of the world's most beautiful squares.

355 Remarkably tall and slim, the Torre del Mangia was added to the body of the Palazzo Pubblico in 1338, with the construction being entrusted to the Perugian brothers Minuccio and Francesco di Rinaldo. The belfry crowning the tower is the work of Lippo Memmi.

LUCCA, TO THE MEMORY OF ILARIA DEL CARRETTO

356 The mosaic on the facade of the church of San Frediano is traditionally attributed to the school of Berlingheri. It depicts the Ascension of Christ and can be read like the illuminated page of a precious medieval missal.

357 The church of San Michele in Foro is located on the former site of the Roman forum. The richly decorated facade is an excellent example of Pisan-Lucchese Romanesque: a perfect thirteenth century scene.

358 top The tomb of Ilaria del Caretto by Jacopo della Quercia lays in the Duomo at Lucca. The young wife of Paolo Guinigi, a nobleman of the city, is portrayed in all her beauty, surrounded by putti and with her favorite dog at her feet. Affection and loss seem to have been perpetuated over the centuries and this is still one of the best loved and most visited monuments.

358 bottom Its uniqueness derives above all from the variety of stylistic, architectural, and decorative features that have been utilized. The marble tiles, the smooth and carved columns, and the asymmetry determined by the successive addition of the campanile all make it a fascinatingly original work.

358-359 The Duomo at Lucca, dedicated to San Martino, has a long and glorious history stretching back to the era of San Frediano in the sixth century. It was later rebuilt by Anselmo di Baggio, but assumed its definitive form in the thirteenth century.

PISA, WEALTH AND CULTURE IN THE SHADOW OF THE TOWER

360 Behind the Duomo stands the Campanile, the Leaning Tower. Medieval records reveal that the tower soon gave cause for concern and that attempts to compensate for the subsidence began at the end of the thirteenth century.

360-361 Pisa's magnificent monumental complex, the Duomo, the Tower, the Baptistery, and the Camposanto, bears witness to the historic wealth of the city. The fate of the campanile, which has always suffered from the effects of subsidence, has the world holding its breath.

361 bottom Buscheto's genius, said to be responsible for the Duomo at Pisa (the photo shows a detail of the apse), developed in an ambient rich in classical references, open to the influence of Eastern culture and extremely advanced from a technological point of view.

362 The shapely dome of the Duomo at Pisa rests on a high tambor and is considered to be the first example of an "extradosal dome." Like the cathedral itself, it is thought to be the work of Buscheto who rests in a tomb located below one of the arcades of the facade.

363 The vibrant chiaroscuro typical of the Pisan arcades is developed in a thousand different ways on the monuments of the Piazza dei Miracoli.

364-365 Lined by sober palazzi, the banks of the Arno at Pisa are symbolic of the composed dignity of the city as the great river prepares to conclude at the Tyrrhenian Sea a journey begun on the Falterona uplands.

MASSA, CARRARA AND LIVORNO, CITIES OF MARBLE

366 top Even the palazzi that stand in the center of Massa speak of a pomp and wealth that reflect the glorious past of the town.

366 bottom Capital of the Duchy of Massa and Carrara in the sixteenth century, prior to the eleventh century Massa was just a small rural center which only developed following the decline of the nearby Luni. It first belonged to the Malaspina family of Fosdinova, and then the Cybo-Malaspina family who gave it its definitive plan. Massa Cybea, with a regular grid plan, saw the building of palazzi and churches, and above all the large red palazzo which in the eighteenth century was decorated with stucco, grotesque carvings, and floral motifs.

367 top The Mastio di Matilde shows above the massive walls of the Fortezza Vecchia at Livorno. It dates back to the eleventh century, but its origins go even further back. It was built on the site of Roman ruins in the first century before Christ.

367 bottom The imposing Porto Mediceo at Livorno was built between 1571 and 1618. The port benefited from a system of duty-free re-exportation of goods held in bond. In 1675 it was declared a free port, a move which increased the prosperity of the city on the Tyrrhenian Sea. To the right runs the sea front. It recalls Leghorn's past maritime splendors with the opulent grace of the Umbertine buildings lightened by the esplanades and terraces facing the open sea.

SAN GIMIGNANO, ANCIENT SYMBOL OF POWER

368 and 369 Thanks to its strategic position clinging to a hillside dominating the Val d'Elsa on the Via Francigena, in the Middle Ages San Gimignano enjoyed a golden age. But the rivalry between the various noble families, in particular the Ardinghelli Guelphs and the Ghibelline Salvucci, led to the explosion of tragically bloody struggles. The towers were thus in reality veritable fortresses set one in front of the other: a memento of past splendors but also of tragedy and mourning.

CYPRESSES, VILLAS AND VILLAGES

Set between the Alps and Sicily, between North and South, featuring mountains and hills, open valleys and narrow gorges, Tuscany is more than just art. Tuscany is countryside so characteristic that the phrase "a Tuscan landscape" is also used to describe that of Umbria or the Marche. The Chianti hills, the Sienese Crete, the Mugello, the Maremma, and the Garfagnana are not simply ideal backdrops to a thousand towns and villages. They are an indispensable part of their appeal, inseparable from the work of man.

There was a strong temptation to start to describe the least cherished, most mistreated and overlooked area, the bleak Maremma. Instead, it joins the narrative after taking leave of Tuscany from the haven of Monte Argentario after having been welcomed by the Mugello, an immense lake of green forests bordered by the Apennines and crowned by Monte Falterona, source of the "fiumicel" as Dante called the Arno. Entering Tuscany by this route must have gladdened the hearts of the travellers of bygone times. It is a landscape of hills, knolls, villas, and fortresses, the favored retreat of the Florentines who, from the late fourteenth century, had astutely swept away the feudal strongholds of the Guidi and the Albertini, transforming the Val di Sieve into an oasis of peace. The Medici were originally from this area and indulged themselves in such idle pursuits as hunting and feasting. The proximity and dominance of Florence also deprived the Mugello of its native heroes. Few now remember that Giotto, Fra Angelico, and Andrea del Castagno were from the Mugello, eternally annexed as they are by the city. It is of some consolation to visit regal villas like that at Cafaggiolo, built for Cosimo il Vecchio near Barberino, or the village of Scarperia, famous for its knife-making crafts. One then moves on through Fiorenzuola, with its "Rocca," or fortress, and city walls designed by Sangallo, to Borgo San Lorenzo, the "capital" of the Mugello. An ancient castle dedicated more to commerce than to defence (it still hosts a lively weekly market), and featuring the superlative "Pieve" (parish church) di San Lorenzo which boasts a Madonna attributed to Giotto. The Mugello extends almost infinitely into a landscape full of color which brings one to Vespignano, considered to be the birthplace of Giotto and said to be the site of his historic meeting with Cimabue, and to Vicchio, home of Fra Angelico. It is certainly not difficult to imagine a scene so crucial to the history of art set among the "pievi," the hills punctuating the route towards Dicomano. This is the land of painters in which the style that made Florence great was formed and nurtured. The woods make marvelous rambling country and one can clamber up the knolls in the hope of spying a hidden monastery, or one of the rare castles to have survived to the present day. Lost sensations are there to be discovered among the myriad shades of green which vary with the seasons.

To the south of the Mugello the Casentino extends in an almost unbroken sweep, straddling the border between Tuscany and Emilia. This is the upper Arno valley, and Dante was the first to remark on its impressive beauty and cool climate, so different to the torrid heat of Florence. However, despite its pleasant appearance, the tempestuous battles which have over the centuries shattered its tranquillity, certainly did not escape the poet's notice. The very name of the Campaldino plain, theater of the victory of the Florentine Guelphs over the Ghibellines of Arezzo, or that of Anghiari is sufficient to evoke memories of pain and blood. Fortunately, this is also a land of great artists, from Piero della Francesca to Michelangelo to Paolo Uccello, and great spirituality.

Monte della Verna, for example, belonged to an incorrigible medieval Don Juan, Orlando Cattani of Siena, who could hardly have dreamed that an insignificant, ragged monk would overturn his life. The monk in question was Francis of Assisi, visiting the San Leo castle in Romagna. Orlando heard him speak, was converted, and subsequently presented him with the entire mountain.

Francis and his followers, with the help of their benefactor, raised a church on La Verna where he later received the stigmata. Today the Verna Sanctuary is a monastery, library, museum, and even a meteorological observatory.

The origins of the Camaldoli monastery also lie in a story of patronage. On this occasion, the protagonist was San Romualdo, who a little after the year 1000 was given permission by Maldolo of Arezzo to build on the ruins of a castle.

374-375 Set among the rolling Sienese hills is the church of San Biagio, designed by Antonio da Sangallo the Elder. The golden travertine stone stets off the harmonious simplicity of the building set on a knoll below the town of Montepulciano.

375 A few miles out of Siena, the Castello delle Quattro Torri stands in magnificent isolation. Built between the fourteenth and fifteenth centuries, the castle is very similar to the Este family's castle at Ferrara built at around the same time.

376-377 The Val d'Orcia frequently offers panoramas like this one: gentle, rolling hills crowned by an occasional cypress grove silhouetted against the skyline.

378-379 Man has always intervened to model, delimit, and render more fertile the Tuscan countryside. In the area around Siena even the rural dwellings are magically integrated into the landscape.

The monks of Camaldoli were fundamental to the diffusion of knowledge in the Middle Ages. Locked into their hermitage, bound by a severe order, they copied codices long before the advent of the printed word simplified matters, and in the early sixteenth century they founded an important press. Immersed in the woods, La Verna and Camaldoli are true oases of peace. Art, on the other hand, is to be found in the numerous towns and villages, with due homage being paid to Pratovecchio, birthplace of Paolo Uccello, and the neighboring parish of Romena, the most important in the Casentino valley. One should also pause at Poppi, the favorite residence of the Guidi family.

The Castello dei Guidi, an evocative remnant of the Middle Ages, is a still formidable symbol of secular feudalism, and it makes one wonder what impact its bulk may have had on the enemy forces. It would appear, in fact, that the Palazzo della Signoria in Florence is a simple copy, even though there are those who claim that the current flowed in the opposite direction and that it was the victors who

exported their style to the area. The last stop is at Cortona, a fascinating city to say the very least, blessed by an invaluable artistic heritage and virtually unchanged from the Renaissance to the present day. First and foremost, there is the magnificent Santa Maria al Calcinaio, then San Domenico, embellished with superb paintings, the Duomo, the remains of the Etruscan fortifications, the Palazzo Pretorio, and the Museo Diocesano. Even a stroll along the paved streets, browsing in the antique shops, can be enchanting as one is transported back in time. Tuscany can also be entered via other mountains, such as the Lunigiana overlooking the baroque, medieval town of Pontremoli with its old houses with slate roofs and the splendid castle housing the archaeological museum, custodian of the Luni civilization. The statue-like stele pose countless unresolved mysteries. Were they idols? Marker stones? Funeral stones? No one knows. Curiosity is combined with unease in this portion of land which is Tuscan in name, but which still retains something of Emilia and Liguria. Descending from Pontremoli towards the sea along the road halfway up the hillside, to the right the landscape is dark and brooding, while to the left are the sunny "pievi" and castles. This was a tempestuous region with around 30 castles, and over 150 fortified houses and watchtowers. However, it has redeemed itself admirably with culture. The Bancarella literary prize, awarded each summer in the Piazza della Repubblica

in Pontremoli, is an event crucial to taking the pulse of Italian readers, while the booksellers' town par excellence is Montereggio, immersed deep in the countryside. The inhabitants of this valley have roamed the world for four centuries founding book shops and publishing companies. The area is under the jurisdiction of the Massa-Carrara province. While Massa is a prevalently modern town, albeit with a historic medieval nucleus huddled around the fortress, Carrara is synonymous with marble, and not only in Italy. For centuries the precious material on which entire pages of the history of art have been written has been extracted from the quarries in the Carrione valley. Marble has been the source of the area's wealth for at least two thousand years, and the entire Apuane landscape bears the scars of mining, furrowed as it is by the canyons and by the white blazes of the waste tips. A blessing for the economy of the area, but one which Carrara has paid for in terms of an industrial appearance, redeemed by the occasional attractive seventeenth-century palazzo, and above all by the Romanesque-Gothic Duomo.

Leaving the city behind, one climbs the steeply twisting roads towards Colonnata or Fantiscritti, and from the road one can see the great scars where Michelangelo quarried the marble for the statues in the Medici chapels and the tomb of Julius II.

From here, passing by way of the Pian della Foiba, one enters the Garfagnana where, much against his will, Ariosto spent unhappy years as Governor on behalf of the Estes. Narrow valleys dense with oaks

380-381 and 380 bottom The villages of Colonnata and Torano serve the surrounding marble quarries. Set like outcrops in a rocky landscape, they have always been tied to these rich yet grudging mountains which concede their wealth only to those with the expertise to mine their slopes of white gold.

381 The marble quarries which dominate the village of Campo Cecina on the Apuane hills have supplied the material on which immortal pages in the history of art have been written for two thousand years.

lead to Castelnuovo, Coreglia Antelminelli, Bagni di Lucca, and the delights of Barga, beloved of Giovannino Pascoli, and on to the Grotta del Vento, which works wonders for the lungs. Here great art is diluted by the domestic familiarity of the poetry learnt by heart in Italian primary schools, and the memory of a well-known and much maligned poet. But each village has a Romanesque church, a terracotta, a crucifix, or a pulpit worthy of a visit. On occasion, as in 1994, one may have the good fortune to come across a relic of the past which has survived

382 top The ruins of the Abbazia di San Galgano, set in the midst of the countryside, are one of the most evocative Romanesque monuments in the Sienese area.

382 bottom The Abbazia di Monte Oliveto Maggiore houses superb frescoes by Luca Signorelli and Sodoma, considered to be among the most important works of the Renaissance.

intact. When Lake Vagli, created by a hydroelectric dam, was drained, the drowned village of Fabbriche di Careggine reappeared. The mute roads, the roofless church, and the abandoned houses came back to life for a few months before being submerged once more in the tranquil silence of the Garfagnana. One descends rapidly from the Apuane mountains to the plain and then to the sea. First the Versilia coast where the old fishing villages of Forte dei Marmi, le Focette, Pietrasanta, Camaiore, and Viareggio have become part and parcel of the summer entertainment industry, while often retaining something of their aristocratic detachment. Following the coast one enters the territory beloved of Puccini, Torre del Lago, the expanse of Lake Massciuccoli and the wonderful presidential estate of San Rossore. After just a few miles, however, the green pine woods give way to the port of Livorno, also known as Leghorn in English. For those not born here, this is a difficult city to love. Built facing the sea but simply, without drama, uncompromisingly "un-Tuscan," and with no attractive quarters, its lack of impressive structures is perhaps due in part to its uniform layout (and its relative youth). Reliable records of its existence date back no further than the fourteenth century when a miniscule fishing village existed on the site where the Medicean port was to be founded. The vicissitudes of the city, among which was a brief period of subjection to Genoa, had had little effect until 1530 when, under the dominion of the Medici, Livorno became the most important port in Tuscany. Its demographic expansion began in the seventeenth century. The city attracted considerable immigration both from the rest of Grand Duchy and from abroad, and it guaranteed religious freedom for all.

This was a truly remarkable act and made Livorno one of the few earthly "paradises" for Jews, a situation unique in Italy which was to last until the age of Napoleon I, and which saw the birth of great "leshivòths" and even its own language, Bagito.

The great synagogue, considered to be among the most beautiful in Italy, was destroyed and it has recently been replaced with an unremarkable temple.

The fame of Livorno as the city of freedom began to grow from the seventeenth century. The foreign population soon reached 35% of the total.

Great political ferment was also stimulated in a similar fashion, thanks to industrial development which from the nineteenth century concentrated an increasingly numerous proletariat around the port. Livorno is the city of the International Workers Association, the Universal Democratic Alliance, the Bacunian Anarchists and the Socialist Congress

382-383 For some years now the Abbazia di Sant'Antimo has once again echoed to the sound of Gregorian chants thanks to five French monks who have dedicated themselves to the order and the upkeep of the abbey.

383 bottom The wealthy Abbazia di Monte Oliveto Maggiore, one of the grandest in Tuscany, looks out over the Sienese Crete. The abbey was founded in 1313 by Giovanni Tolomei, a master of Law at the Sienese Studio who abandoned wealth and honor in favor of a Benedictine monastic life with a special interest in art and science.

384 Sadly, typical rural dwellings in the Val d'Orcia are occasionally allowed to fall into disrepair. For some years now, however, the cottages have become the preferred prey of both Italians and foreigners who buy and restore them to an oasis of holiday peace and tranquility.

385 Monteriggioni (left) and Certaldo (right): two diverse destinies for two medieval villages with important roles in history and literature. Monteriggioni, isolated on a hill top, supports itself in its splendid decline through tourism and nostalgia, virtually shunning any contact with modernity. Certaldo, the birthplace of Francesco Boccaccio, has on the other hand adapted with the times to become an important industrial center.

which, in 1921, saw the birth of the Italian Communist Party. The inhabitants of Livorno still retain a reputation for being less than peaceful, but ever ready for a joke. It is worth recalling the ferocious trick pulled by three students just a few years ago when they totally hoodwinked massed ranks of experts with their claims that the fragments of stone they had modeled with an electric drill were actually original Modigliani sculptures. The whole world laughed and Livorno applauded. Tricking their neighbors, taking pride in their own individuality, well removed from the other Tuscans with even their own dialect, they are contrary to nature in these parts. Even though it is some distance away, well off shore and down a bit towards the south, the Tuscan archipelago also belongs to the province of Livorno. The seven islands of varying sizes are the summits of seven Apennine peaks, submerged and separated from the mainland millions of years ago, although legend would have it that they were created when the necklace of the Venus of Tyrrhene broke, scattering the gems of which it was composed. Those precious stones gave rise to Elba, Gorgona, Capraia, Pianosa, Montecristo, Giglio, and Giannutri.

It is said that Jason during his wanderings with Medea sailed into the bay of Elba where today stands the port of Portoferraio. Elba was in fact well known in ancient times when the Ligurians and the Greeks exploited its iron ore deposits a thousand years before Christ. The Romans, on the other hand, were more interested in its wines, even though Virgil described it as "insula inexhaustis chalybum generosa metallis." Iron and "tourism" have thus alternated in the economic and political history of Elba up to the present day, with the significant historical interlude of the 300-day imprisonment of Napoleon.

More isolated, and perhaps still more fascinating, the other islands have enjoyed diverse destinies. They have often been the refuges of monks, hermits, and lovers of silence, meditation, and prayer, as can be seen from the ruins of the small monasteries left on Giannutri and the magnificent Montecristo, but also the strongholds of the various conquerors to have alternated over the course of the centuries, from Pisa to the Appians to the Medici. Montecristo, where Dumas set Edmond Dantès' hunt for treasure, is

386-387 Sorano, in the province of Grosseto, dominates the Lente valley from a rocky spur. The compact village center retains a markedly medieval character, exemplified by the tower-houses and the imposing Fortezza Ursinea.

388-389 Pitigliano also perches on an outcrop of tuff, and a fine white wine is produced on the surrounding hills. In the past the village housed a large Jewish community.

390 top Montepulciano (in the photo, the Palazzo del Comune) is one of the most typical sixteenth century towns. Its appearance was radically changed by the work of Antonio da Sangallo, with significant contributions also made by Michelozzo and Vignola. On a smaller scale, the Palazzo del Comune is inspired by the style of the Palazzo Vecchio in Florence.

390 center The current form of the ancient Vallambrosana abbey of Passignano, near Tavernelle Val di Pesa, dates back to the seventeenth century. The interior is decorated with works by Cresti, Alessandro Allori, Butteri, and Veli.

390 bottom On an isolated knoll on the slopes of the Chianti region stands the magnificent Castello di Brolio, home to one of the most famous wine producers of the area, Ricasoli. It was Bettino Ricasoli, an expert in agricultural matters, who invented the Chianti "formula": a blend of Sangiovese, Trebbiano, Malvasia, and Canaiolo grapes.

391 In the small, evocative village of Collodi, birthplace of Carlo Lorenzetti, the author of Pinocchio, Villa Garzoni stands out as an ideal model of the aristocratic villa, complemented by a garden begun in the mid-sixteenth century by Marquis Romano Garzoni and perfected in the seventeenth century by Ottaviano Diodati.

today a protected wildlife reserve after having once been the private hunting grounds of Vittorio Emanuele II. All the islands are veritable natural paradises, from Pianosa, a tormenting source of anguish for convicts, to the volcanic rocks of Capraia and the gentle beaches of Giglio which alternate with stretches of rugged cliffs. Their destiny has always been that of the struggle between exploitation and the perhaps unconfessed desire to remain detached, beautiful, and isolated, almost untouchable.

Returning to the mainland, and moving away from the sea on the road towards Siena, the underground wealth of the area once again takes pride of place. Between the Cecina and Ombrone valleys extend the Colline Metallifere (the Metal Hills) with names which all evoke the fires of hell. The Luciferian blow-holes of Larderello lend the landscape a lunar aspect, and the ancients were convinced that the snorts came straight from the depths of Hades. Today the cylinders of the cooling towers and the steel pipework conceal much of the natural phenomena. Fortunately Volterra is close by, "an eagle's nest in precarious equilibrium," isolated among hills that concealed treasure: copper, lead, silver, and rock salt.

Volterra was already important in Etruscan times, the ancient Velathri, one of the twelve "lucomonie," with huge, imposing walls, traces of which still remain. The Middle Ages, on the other hand, saw the city clinging to its castle, huddled around the Piazza dei Priori. But thanks to the underground resources and its strategic position, it was destined to succumb to the power of the neighboring cities. As usual, Florence triumphed and immediately imposed its presence installing the bulky Fortress, used as a prison. Volterra resigned itself to its destiny and it still appears to be waiting for its destiny to be fulfilled today. In the surrounding area, the phenomena of landslides on the hillsides, the dreaded "Balze," have already swallowed up cemeteries, villages, and Etruscan walls. An ancient Camaldolese abbey of Saints Justus and Clemente is now threatened, while another, now abandoned, is awaiting its fate. The future of the Chianti appears more tranquil. It is a region embodying the very essence of natural harmony in which man's activities are integrated in perfect symbiosis.

It enchants with its undulating hills patchworked by vineyards, cultivated fields and farms, and punctuated by avenues of cypresses, villages, and valleys which take their names from the rivers running through them. The mosaic proves unforgettable and unmistakable for anyone granted even the most fleeting of glimpses. The Florentine nobility retreated to the Val di Pesa for their vacations, and in the area around San Casciano, at Sant'Andrea in Percussina, Machiavelli found a haven from the cares of politics, dining with the local dignitaries: the baker, the notary, the miller, and the innkeeper. He enjoyed simple life favored by the climate, the greenery, and the shade of the cypress avenues. Val d'Elsa also appears suited to idleness with its knolls and the harmonious profiles of its hills. And yet, it is not lacking in memorials to proud combative moments. Boccaccio, born here at Certaldo, said that the waters of the Elsa had the property of turning bodies to stone and that it was dangerous to immerse oneself in them. What is certain is that along its course have arisen cities of stone.

San Gimignano is famed for its towers, although few remain compared with the seventy-odd which are said to have graced the town during its golden age.

San Gimignano was an important and wealthy trading point on the Via Francigena and in spite of its current decadence it remains one of Tuscany's historic sites, not only for its artistic treasures but also for that perfect landscape, that view which from

392-393 There are numerous villas throughout Tuscany, some in rural settings like this one near Radda in Chianti, surrounded by vineyards, others in more markedly aristocratic surroundings. They are all, however, harmoniously inserted into the landscape and have, over the course of time, become an integral part of it.

392 bottom The Medici enjoyed the peaceful country life, especially when it was enlivened by feasting and sparkling conservation. The villas at Artimino (left) by Buontalenti and Poggio a Caiano (right) by Giuliano da Sangallo were among the favorites of the Florentine gentry.

on high extends in all directions, encompassing hills, villages, and meadows. There is no rhetoric in saying that here Father Time hesitated, undecided as to whether to proceed or to freeze, immobile.

The two triangular piazzas, Piazza Cisterna and Piazza Duomo, are indispensable openings in a maze of streets and tall buildings, and feature the Collegiata (with frescos by Benozzo Gozzoli and Taddeo di Bartolo, and the Annunciation by Jacopo della Quercia), the Palazzo della Podestà, and two important museums with collections of masterpieces

393 Villa La Peggio, near Grassina, was acquired by Francesco I de'Medici in 1569, but it was Cardinal Francesco Maria, brother of the Grand Duke Cosimo III, who made it the theater of feasting and receptions celebrated by poets of the era such as Giovanni Battista Faginoli and Francesco Redi.

of Florentine and Sienese art. San Gimignano is the
most enchanting welcome to the Val d'Elsa
imaginable, but it is not the only attraction. It is but
a short drive to Colle Val d'Elsa, another product of
the wealth created by the Via Francigena, but one
with a rather different vocation. Only a fragment of
the medieval town remains, set high above in contrast
to the more "modern" section below. Further down
the valley, ever since the Middle Ages, a network of
canals has carried water to the wool and paper mills.

The wealthy and faithful Colle made no great

drama out of submitting to the might of Florence and
continued to prosper and enrich itself with works of
art. A completely different destiny awaited
Monteriggioni, a village virtually straddling the
border between Val d'Elsa and the Chianti hills. It
was early in the thirteenth century when the Sienese
decided to acquire a small hill from the nobility of
Staggia in order to create a fortress capable of
intimidating the omnipresent Florentines. This was a
large, forbidding castle for its time, with a closed ring
of stone, reinforced by fourteen towers. It is still awe-

395 There is more to the
Chianti than just vineyards.
There are also hidden
monasteries and old country
houses immersed in the
luxuriant greenery. This
location is close to Castellina,
between the Pesa and Staggia
valleys.

396-397 In the Balze
of Volterra, the sudden
shifting of the clayey ground,
has over time swallowed up
churches, houses, and
convents. Today many
historic buildings are still
threatened by seemingly
inevitable destruction.

inspiring today, so isolated and brooding, protected
by the Romanesque-Gothic church dedicated to Our
Lady of the Assumption. From the peak of the hill one
looks out over the Chianti hills, that marvelous
synthesis of nature and the work of man, where even
agriculture appears graced by art. The rural homes
have an enchanting simplicity, and even the roads
trace patterns far removed from the usual anonymous
grids. The landscape has been modeled since the
Middle Ages, adapting terrain that was not always so
gently accommodating, such as the already mentioned
"Balze" in the Volterra region, and beyond Siena, the
Crete that occasionally degenerate into a harsh, lunar
ruggedness. The Chianti region is thus not so
uniform as one might think, although it is possible to
clearly define the Chianti Classico wine producing
area, which includes the Arbia, Pesa, and Greve
valleys as far as the Val d'Orcia. The area does have
an identifying symbol however: the cypresses which
dot the countryside, emphasize the ridges of the hills,
and appear in the paintings of the great artists.
Cypresses and vineyards, fortresses, castles, villages,

398 Close to Coreglia Antelminelli, a famous holiday retreat in the Garfagnana, there are numerous small villages which appear to be as close to the past as they are to the present day, surrounded by the dense green woodlands.

398-399 The Turrite stream in the Garfagnana flows past the village of Turrite Secca. Harsh and isolated, the area can throw up unexpected oases of greenery in the valleys between the high rocky mountains.

"pievi," and abbeys: even an elementary list of the attractions would be lengthy. The suggestive area around Sovicille, for example, is rich in "pievi," castles, villages, and villas. On the rounded hills of the Sienese Montagnola there are spiritual havens such as the Agostinian hermitages at Lecceto and San Leonardo al Lago, or the beautiful Romanesque church at Ponte allo Spino. Not far away, the Romanesque style is again in magnificent evidence in the grandiose, solitary and imposing Sant'Antimo abbey, a few miles from Montalcino.

The abbey appears at the foot of a valley like a mirage, lovingly cared for by five French monks who fervently practice the Gregorian rite. Those visitors who wish to experience the illusion of time travel can take part in the services. The sung mass on Sunday is not to be missed. Just as evocative are the San Galgano Abbey, the ruins of which are to be found open to the sky in the midst of the countryside, and

the fortified abbey of Monte Oliveto, set in the Sienese Crete and surrounded by a dense cloak of hollies and cypresses. Luca Signorelli left an imposing memorial to art here as did Sodoma.

The entire area is rich in artistic testimony. Above all there is Pienza, "born out of a idea of love and a dream of beauty," as Pascoli wrote. It was Pope Pius II, Aenea Silvyus Piccolomini, who had the inspired, insane idea of transforming his birthplace, the little village of Corsignano, into a Renaissance utopia, the ideal city.

Thanks to Leon Battista Alberti and Bernardo Rossellino, in just three years the dream became reality. The old medieval layout was swept away, and space was made for the cathedral, with a plain, bare interior so as not to interfere with its architectural perfection, and Palazzo Piccolomini with its loggia overlooking the Val d'Orcia. All this took place while a few miles away the Romanesque and Gothic styles continued to hold sway at, for example, the minute and wholly delightful village of San Quirico or at Montalcino, the home of the Brunello, the most noble

399 bottom From Barga, the artistic jewel of the Garfagnana, one can look out over the lush countryside punctuated by rustic cottages. Among its treasures the village boasts the beloved house of Giovanni Pascoli, a precious example of the privileged bourgeois lifestyle of the last century.

400-401 "The serenity of the air settled over everything like a morning dew," wrote Federigo Tozzi about the Sienese countryside which nothing seems to disturb.

402-403 The bell tower of Monte Oliveto Maggiore seems to emerge directly from the fog that mantles the Sienese hills.

and expensive of Italian wines, a veritable nectar for the disciples of Bacchus. A visit to one of the cellars is a must. The owners are usually only too happy to offer a taste of the fruit of painstakingly tended and precious vineyards. Wine shops abound along the remarkably evocative streets of the town. Each bottle, each vintage, each label is a discovery in its own right. Not far from Montalcini lies another compact surprise, Bagno Vignoni, where the principal piazza is an open-air thermal "piscina." Lorenzo il Magnifico and Pius II came here to treat their rheumatism. The village has been saved from a project which would have transformed it into a form of Tuscan Disneyland, but like many other villages of incomparable beauty in the region it risks being abandoned.

This is not the case at Montepulciano, which thanks to its strategic position between the Florentine Republic, the States of the Church, and Siena,

succeeded in forging artistic influences fundamental to its economic and urban development and became a splendid Renaissance city.

The symbol of the town is its magnificent pilgrimage church of the Madonna di San Biagio by Antonio da Sangallo il Vecchio, situated on a knoll where legend has it that the Virgin Mary appeared before two children and a shepherd in 1518. The name of Montepulciano is also known throughout the world thanks to its Vino Nobile, one of the seven guaranteed quality Italian wines. It is but a short step

406 Giannutri, the southernmost of the islands in the Tuscan archipelago, features the notable remains of a large Roman villa which perhaps belonged to the Domizi Enobarbi family. Roman remains have also been found on the sea bed below the crystal clear water.

406-407 Elba, the largest of the islands in the Tuscan archipelago, was held by the Etruscans, the Greeks, the Romans, and the Lombards before passing to the Republic of Pisa. Its destiny has been determined by its beauty, its strategic position, and also by its considerable natural resources.

407 bottom left Mediterranean maquis thrives on the rocks of the island of Giglio, alternating with minuscule sandy beaches.

from the wealth of the Chianti hills to the Maremma, a harsh region, maltreated and often overlooked.

One first has to traverse Monte Amiata, the Mountain of Caves as the Romans called it because of its porous nature and abundant springs. It rises in isolation, an extinct volcano where the Quaternary deposits of the siliceous shells of diatoms are extracted in the form of a fossil flour or "moon milk." Deep in the heart of the mountain mercury can also be found. The springs of Amiata supply Siena, Grosseto, and the whole of southern Tuscany down to Viterbo. The mountain is manna for the grim Maremma and its "capital" Grosseto, something of the Cinderella of Tuscan cities, obscured even by the neighboring Massa Marittima. This is in spite of the presence of massive fortified city walls, a monumental complex which has earned Grosseto a reputation as a minor version of Lucca, an honor for a city which prior to improvements was considered so unattractive that to live there was considered a form of punishment.

It is probably not widely known that up to the last century the public offices of the "lower province of Siena" were transferred to Scansano in the summer months. This was the so-called "estatura," a prudent migration to avoid an epidemic of malaria among the loyal civil servants. In an even earlier age convicts were faced with a choice: imprisonment in the Maschio at Volterra, or forced labor in the Maremma, and the freedom to die of malaria.

There followed bombardments and subsequent reconstruction which, over the course of a few

407 bottom right Capraia, standing a long way out from the coast (one of the reasons for which it was chosen as a penal colony), attracted arrows of Dante's ire against the Pisan gentlemen.

decades, has increased the original dimensions of the city fifteen-fold. It is worth pausing, at least for a while, if only to look at the ruins which bear testimony to the succession of masters and peoples: the Etruscan walls, the Roman basilica, and the paleochristian cathedral. One can walk around the ring of green created within the fortified walls in the first half of the nineteenth century, a meeting place but also a dividing line between the humble and generally unloved Grosseto of the "estatura" and the modern city of tower blocks and chaotic planning.

408-409 The island of Capraia is of extreme geological interest and is generally composed of volcanic rocks with flows of andesite, tufa, breccia, and basaltic rocks. Its name derives from the wild goats found there.

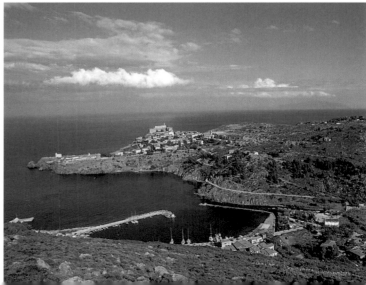

410 and 411 *These are the butteri, the cowboys or gauchos of Italy. Almost inseparable from their horses and the herds they tend, they were once the kings of the Maremma but condemned to labor in a harsh climate, infested with malaria, the curse of the area up until the last century.*

The butteri still survive and at the village fairs, or at branding time one can see that they are still as rugged as they were at the beginning of the twentieth century when they successfully met the challenge of the legendary Buffalo Bill, touring Italy at the time.

412-413 *The Alberese pine forest was at one time a Sienese fief and source of salt. Only following land reclamation were the now flourishing domestic and maritime pines planted. Today there are over 80,000 trees, separated from the sea by just a slim strip of sand.*

412 bottom In the maze of vegetation which characterizes the Maremma Natural Park, the wild boar, the King of the Maquis, still reigns. One can also find traces of the last remaining wild cats, as well as porcupines, lynxes, pheasants, foxes, and weasels.

413 bottom In the Maremma National Park visitors must stay on the paths so as not to invade the realm of the deers and the wild animals.

414-415 The mouth of the Ombrone is the last bastion of the swamps which once guaranteed the Maremma's infamy as an area of mourning and malaria.

The Maremma of bygone days must have been very different, linked to the Amiata by just two roads, and branded by two contrasting curses, drought and stagnant water. Today's Maremma, on the other hand, has been healed and reclaimed and is an upper echelon tourist destination.

To tell the truth, the tourists tend to steer clear of the interior, with the exception of Capalbio, a haven for intellectuals and politicians. And yet this is not just a land of "butteri" and parched plains, it is also one of Etruscan remains. Populonia, Rusellae, Vetulonia, and Saturnia are only the most well known centers. And while man's negligence has been responsible for dreadful disasters, the tumulus and aedicule tombs, the interiors, and the environs are infinitely suggestive.

The area also boasts its own cities of art such as Pitigliano and Sorano, the cities of tufa, which under the dominion of the Orsini boasted imposing fortifications, and above all Sovana, with its necropolis and the Tomba Ildebranda.

One leaves Tuscany via two protected oases. The Maremma Natural Park, constituted in 1975, extends for around 12 miles along the coast from Tombolo to Talamone, and represents a perfect opportunity to get to know the primitive Maremma.

More than simply a green lung, the ancient watchtowers, the remains of the San Rabano monastery, and the estates where the heirs to the "butteri" continue to raise livestock and horses bear witness to a living territory, one in which man exists in contact and in symbiosis with nature. Nature is again the protagonist at the Orbetello Oasis on the salty lagoon with dunes covered with dense Mediterranean maquis, fresh water ponds, and woods. Here the Knight of Italy, egrets, and occasionally flamingos all nest, and you may also spot the nests of the bee-eater.

At dusk, the dunes taken on a reddish hue in Argentario in the beautiful village of Porto Ercole. This is a chance for a last salute to art. In the parish church below the Rocca is buried Caravaggio who, following an adventurous life in distant parts, came to end his days in the furthest outpost of Tuscany, the homeland of all artists.

IN THE NAME
OF SPORT
AND HONOR

How many of the games, and the traditional customs of the Italian people have become part of the patrimony not just of their city of origin, but the whole country, and perhaps even the world? Very few have but of these few, almost all of them originated in Tuscany. To the prompt of "Siena" a foreigner will probably respond with "Palio," just as "Florence" could be coupled with "Calcio in Costume," and Arezzo with the "Giostra del Saracino." These ancient traditions, to which one could add other events such as Pisa's Gioco del Ponte, or Pistoia's Giostra del'Orso, have often been revived in this century after years of neglect. But the region as a whole is a succession of festivals, often rekindling the competitive spirit of the cities and contrade (neighborhoods) typical of the Middle Ages, and which in the Renaissance was channeled into more relaxed and sporting customs and rituals.

The competitive spirit only rarely spills over into violence, but those watching the "calcio in costume"

in Florence are inevitably obliged to support one or the other of the two factions. Neutrality is outlawed, and so are good manners. And to think that this ball game has the noblest of origins: the "sferomachia," as the Crusca dictionary defines the game, descends directly from the Greeks and the Romans (with all due apologies to the British who believe they invented soccer). The game is documented in Florence as far back as the fifteenth century. It was once usually played in the winter and in 1490 even on the frozen Arno, between the Ponte Vecchio and Santa Trinità.

The ball weighed ten ounces and the costumes were as comfortable as possible to allow freedom of movement. But the most unusual aspect of the sport, at least for that era, was that the participants had no need of arms, crossbows, horses, or lances, but just their feet, and on occasion their hands.

Nowadays the matches are held in Piazza della Signoria between four teams, each representing one of the city's quarters: San Giovanni in green, Santa Croce in blue, Santa Maria Novella in red, and Santo Spirito in white.

416 and 417 There is no holding back for the players in Calcio in Costume in Florence. The match is held in June in Piazza Santa Croce. Four city quarters, San Giovanni, Santa Maria Novella, Santa Croce, and Santo Spirito compete in the games. Although all the participants are called on to swear an oath of fair play, almost anything goes in this intense struggle somewhere between soccer and rugby. And this is despite the fact that the prize is symbolic: a white calf to be eaten all together, as well as the inevitable palio, or banner.

418 The Scoppio del Carro at Florence is all that remains of the tradition of great allegorical floats that lies somewhere between paganism and Christianity and which enjoyed its greatest period during the Renaissance.

418-419 On the night of June 16th Pisa switches off its street lighting and lights oil lamps to celebrate San Ranieri. The following day the city stages the Gioco del Ponte.

The colors are intended to symbolize the four natural elements, the roots and nucleus of everything. Red for fire, green for the land, blue for water and white for air the Calcio in Costume is, in reality, a very early form of rugby. The "rules" allow the tackling of one's opponent, with all the ripping of tunics and more or less underhand blows that entails. For the more inexperienced spectators the confusion increases in relation to the number of players involved, twenty-seven per team including "Datori," "Sconciatori," and "Corridori" (Suppliers, Blockers, and Runners) as well as the "Capitano" and the "Alfiere" (standard bearer).

The chaos often also involves the Maestro di Campo, who has his work cut out to control all fifty-four of the players. The aim of the game is to score points by throwing the ball into the adversary's end zone, thus effecting a "caccia."
A shot at the goal which fails to hit the target results in a half "caccia" for the opposition. And if that seems simple enough, in spite of the "oath of fairness" sworn by the two captains before the start, the matches often deteriorate into saloon-style brawls, with shredded tunics and the dealing of below-the-belt blows accompanied by the roars of the crowd. All that effort is rewarded with a token prize, like all the prizes in these traditional events: a banner and a white calf to be consumed all together at a great banquet.

The origins of Pistoia's Giostra dell'Orso, held in July in honor of San Jacopo, are just as ancient. Originally it was the Palio dei Barberi, a long race through the whole city with a spectacular finish in Piazza del Duomo. It was only following the First World War that the Palio became the Giostra, that is a joust, based above all on skill. The game as it is played today originated in the late 1940's, with considerable historical license being taken. It was even preceded by a rugby match in "primitive" costumes and by a session of mud wrestling. Nowadays the Giostra is held in fifteenth century dress, with much being made of costumed extras, drummers and, flag wavers.

Twelve knights representing the ancient quarters of the city compete on a ring of beaten earth laid down in the piazza as in Siena.

419 bottom The San Ranieri procession at Pisa brings together the faithful from throughout the city in a grandiose illuminated parade rich in emotion, song, and prayer.

The aim is to hit a target in the form of a stylized bear (the same as that which appears in Pistoia's coat of arms) with a lance, trying to get there ahead of one's adversary. It has to be said that even though it has only recently been revived and had suffered long periods of suspension, the Giostra dell'Orso is getting under the skin of the city.

Its inhabitants are rapidly turning into convinced "contradists," perhaps harboring a dream of future glory to match that of Siena with live TV broadcasts and competition among the various networks to secure exclusive rights. Summer is city festival season and Pisa is no exception to the rule. The most passionate and best loved event is that dedicated to the city's patron saint San Ranieri. On the 16th and 17th of August the "Luminaria" lights up the city. On the evening of the 16th the electric street lighting is switched off, and while darkness falls over the city, the banks of the Arno begin to sparkle in the light of thousands of torches.

The torches are suspended on the "biancheria," white-painted wooden supports fixed to the facades of the houses and palazzi. At the same time, thousands of minute boats are loaded with candles and launched on the river to float slowly down towards the sea. The following day the festival explodes when the Santa Maria, Sant'Antonio, San Francesco, and San Martino quarters take their places for a regatta culminating in the oarsmen climbing a long pole on the end of which an embroidered banner is fixed.

The Giostra del Saracino at Arezzo, on the other hand, was not held in honor of a saint. In fact, it was once held to suitably celebrate an important event or to honor an illustrious guest. The revived festival held today differs from the traditional event in that originally any knight could compete, while now the protagonists are the jousters representing the various city quarters. The rituals preceding the event are typical of the various Tuscan palio. In the morning a herald announces the program, followed by a parade of squires and drummers. In the afternoon the arms and the contestants receive the blessing of the parish churches in the various quarters, while the flag wavers perform in Piazza Grande. The actual Giostra is fought by two contestants jousting against an effigy of a Saracen king.

When struck, the effigy swings its lead-weighted whip and the knight has to be ready to dodge its blows. Apart from a few bruises he can also acquire penalty points. The list could go on and on as a giostra, a festival, or a tournament, with more or less reliably documented origins, is held in virtually all Tuscan towns and villages.

However, none of these events could ever hope to exceed the Palio of Siena in terms of fame or excitement. In recent years animal rights activists have railed against the race, fearing maltreatment of the horses, their improper use, and the cruel destiny which, occasionally, leads to them becoming sacrificial victims of the collective passion. The Sienese argue that their foremost interest is the well-being of the steed on which the fate of the contrada rests. After the assignment by ballot, the horses cannot be replaced, and they are treated, spoiled, and watched over like the heir to a throne. One of the contrada's trusted men will sleep in the stall together with the horse. In the three days preceding the race veterinary surgeons are the most sought-after men in the city. Finally, at the end of their career the ageing or injured animals are pensioned off in the beautiful Sienese hills. Arguments apart, everything imaginable has been said and written about the Palio delle Contrade. The rules which govern it, which in their present form date back to the seventeenth century, are severe and it is doubtful whether there is a single Sienese who would want to change the slightest thing. An important role is played by chance which decides which ten of the city's seventeen contrade will participate in the event. And, as we have already seen, it is chance which assigns the horses. The jockey, on the other hand, is chosen, paid and controled by the contrada.

Certain names have become part of Palio legend, such as those of Aceto or Andrea Meloni, winner of the record number of races this century. In the past money was a significant factor as the jockeys were in a position to corrupt their adversaries, but nowadays it appears that the thirst for victory is the ruling passion. The contrada knows how to reward the man responsible for its success. Nevertheless, the role of the jockey is of secondary importance. It is the horse who wins.

421 *The Regata delle Repubbliche Marinare: a celebration of the glorious era in which Pisa contended for domination of the seas against Venice, Genoa, and Amalfi. Only the rivalry remains from the struggles of the past, but it is enough: to arouse the crowd and encourage the participants.*

Its rider may well finish on the floor, thrown against the mattresses padding the fearful San Martino corner. He will receive the necessary treatment, but with no undue sympathy.

This is all part of the intimate internal life of the contrade. The spectators at the Palio see nothing but a riot of colors, sounds, and merrymaking. The festival begins in the morning with a mass celebrated by the archbishop on the Piazza, followed by a rather unenthusiastic trial race. No one wants to risk laming their horse, and rather than gallop,

they trot. Another blessing is given in the afternoon, in the local church of the contrada. The inhabitants all gather round the horse and rider to hear the words of the priest: "Go and return victorious!"

In the meantime the tourists gather in Piazza del Campo. The rich and fortunate sit in the stands or on the balconies while the others squeeze into the arena, trying to cope with the heat, the pushing, and the tension. As the sun slowly begins to set, tingeing the palazzi a deep red, the bells of the

Torre del Mangia ring out and the parade begins to move. It is then the turn of the starter who tries to bring the bareback-ridden horses into line between two ropes before starting the race. It lasts just a few minutes, but those who have seen it even just once remember it as a moment frozen in time in which one struggles even to breathe.

The whole of Siena holds its breath before exploding in a scream of joy or desperation. Sportsmanship has no place here: winning is what counts. Rival contrade do not shake and forget and there are no consoling pats on the back.

They meet up in the evening, however, at great tables to discuss, laugh, and argue. The winning contrada saves a place for the horse too. The other place of honor goes to the palio, the banner painted each year by a different artist, preferably Sienese.

422 and 423 The Maestro di Campo directs the Giostra del Saracino at Arezzo. Once the event was organized to honor illustrious visitors, princes, and sovereigns. Today the contest is between the historic city quarters, Porta Sant'Andrea, Porta Crucifera, Porta del Foro, and Porta Santo Spirito, and is held in Piazza Grande.

SIENA'S SPORT AND SOUL

424 and 425 The flag twirlers, together with the squires, crossbowmen, and pages, participate in the costumed parade preceding the Palio at Siena. It is a great honor for these boys to hurl their contrada's colors into the air. Each contrada has its own colors, traditions, and even museums dedicated to past editions of the Palio in which you can admire precious flags and banners. The illustrations show the emblems of some of the seventeen contrade: Dragon, Giraffe, Hedgehog, Tower, Tortoise, Panther, Wave, Wolf, and Snail.

426 and 427 The Palio at Siena does not last just a few minutes, but a whole year. On the morning of the great day each contrada accompanies the horse which it has been assigned to the parish blessing, before the historical parade in Piazza del Campo. The costumes, the arms, and the decorations are perfect replicas of the medieval items.

428-429 The San Martino corner is the most dangerous. Horses and jockeys often see their races end here to the anguish of their supporters. The mattresses do little to attenuate the pain of defeat.

430 and 431 Three nail-
biting minutes and then one
section of the city explodes
with joy, while the others
despair. The palio, painted
each year by a different artist,
almost always Sienese, is
taken up by the contradists
and kissed, touched, and
praised.

432-433 After all the
trepidation, the winners
celebrate with a great
banquet. The guest of
honor is the horse, the
day's real hero.

434 View of the Turkish Steps in Realmonte.

436-437 Segesta: Greek theater.

438-439 Agrigento: Concordia Temple.

440-441 Etna: volcanic eruption.

a meeting of mediterranean civilizations

SICILY

a meeting of mediterranean civilizations

SICILY

CONTENTS

443 Palermo: Church of Santa Rosalia.

444-445 Calatafimi: Festival of the Crucifix.

446-447 Favignana: tuna killing.

INTRODUCTION

449 Favignana is one of the
few places in Sicily where the
traditional activity of tuna-
fishing, once Sicily's largest
industry, is still carried out.
There used to be twenty- one
tuna processing plants in
Sicily, surrounded by salt-
works that produced the salt
used to conserve the fish.
It is an example of an
economy integrated with
and respectful of nature.

It would certainly be presumptuous to try to
describe Sicily in a single book because even the
smallest of the 420 communes of the island (the largest
region in Italy) has such a vast historical,
architectural, cultural and natural wealth that it alone
would merit a volume. And so as not to reduce this
book to a long and dry series of lists, the only choice
possible is to paint the island with broad brushstrokes, picking out the occasional detail in
discussions of monuments, traditional activities, the
people and their legends in order to give an idea of the
atmosphere of Sicily, the island in which, according to
Johann Wolfgang Goethe, "lies the key to everything."
"Italy without Sicily," wrote the great German at the
end of the 18th century, "leaves no image in the soul."
And one cannot but share Goethe's feeling if one
considers that this island represented not the
demarcation line but the point of contact and fusion of
many Mediterranean cultures. It is, in Goethe's
words, "a marvellous center where the many spokes of
universal history converge."

What makes Sicily fascinating is its unique blend
of cultures and races created by the lure, since
prehistoric times, of its mild climate, fertile land and
strategic position. Many peoples were induced to
climb aboard this enormous ship berthed at the center
of the Mediterranean; of the native people, we know
almost nothing except for the remains in the cave of
Uzzo and those, even more ancient, of a delicate race
of Australopithecus hominids that lived in the area
around Agrigento between five million and three and
a half million years ago when Sicily was still attached
to Tunisia. Apart from the Elimo tribe, the first people
we know of settled beneath the great mountain that
spits flame. These were the Sicans, who probably
reached the island on giant rafts from Iberia. They
chose the area around Mount Etna because the black
sand that spouts from the volcano makes the
surrounding soil so fertile. But 1500 years before
Christ, according to Diodorus, the Sicans fled to the
west of the island as a result of a particularly
frightening eruption. This left space for the Siculi
tribe who arrived from Lazio in mainland Italy several
millennia after the arrival of the Sicani. It was Italo,
king of the Siculi, that the peninsula was named after.
The Siculi (who probably belonged to the same ethnic

group as the Sicani) passed across the Strait of
Messina on skins filled with air and built Sicily's first
metropolis, below the volcano. The remains of the
settlement – encircled by towers, inhabited by 2000
people and boasting a temple dedicated to a god named
Adranon that personified Etna, the lord of fire and
war – can still be seen on the banks of the river
Simeto. It was here that the first and only inscription
in the language of the people who gave their name to
the island has been found. The Siculi also built
Pantalica, Europe's largest prehistoric necropolis
containing 5000 tombs excavated in sheer rock faces.
Excavation must have been a titanic task considering
that they were dug out before the discovery of iron.

Next the Greeks arrived; they built cities, temples
and theaters, they imported olives, pistachios and
vines and enriched the pottery art of the Siculi. Then
there were the Phoenicians who left immense dry-
docks, mosaics and exotic idols. Later, of course, the
Romans arrived. They made the island into an
immense granary and built splendid villas and palaces
adorned with statues. Following the Romans came the
Byzantines, who built Cube and other rock churches
and transformed the sanctuary of Athena into
Syracuse's first cathedral and the Concordia Temple in
Agrigento into a church. The Arabs followed and left a
legacy of mosques, minarets and such lovely Gardens
of Delight that Count Roger the Norman regretted
having destroyed them. The Arabs also created a new
culture of agriculture, cooking and handcrafts; they
divided the island into three valleys and married the
snows of Etna to the juice of citrus fruits and honey to
create delicious sorbets. Following the Normans, the
Swabians arrived. They built hundreds of castles and
towers, some from black lava, and strengthened the
local wines by teaching the islanders how to cultivate
the vines on the faces of the hills most exposed to the
sun.

Then the French – the Angevins – arrived once
more. With them the Gothic architecture of the
Chiaramonte family flourished, prompting the
construction of Palazzo Steri in Palermo but also
causing the famed Sicilian Vespers War. The
Aragonese from Spain became the dominant power.
They married Catalan Gothic to Chiaramonte Gothic
and introduced Baroque architecture when rebuilding

towns destroyed by earthquakes. Their versions of religious ceremonies also left a lasting mark on local Catholic rites. Centuries later, the English arrived. They neither invaded nor colonized; their only aim was to produce port on Sicilian soil and thus they created the Marsala wine district in western Sicily. Finally, the Americans moved into the NATO bases in eastern Sicily, on the heels of jazz and John Wayne movies.

The result is that today Sicily is like an amazing machine that can take you back and forth in time and space: to the dawn of the human world via a volcanic eruption, to prehistoric tombs from 5000 years ago, to an exotic scene like that of the papyrus on the river Ciane, to the snowy silver firs in the Petralian hills. Modern Sicilians are the result of this rich social mix from the past, also of peoples who have come to the island seeking refuge in more recent times, for example, the Albanians who fled during the 15th century in the face of a Turkish invasion and created a community in which their ancient rites are still handed down; and descendants of Lombards called by Count Roger to an area between Etna and the Nebrodi hills that still speak an ancient Gallic-Italian dialect. All these peoples exist within the traditions and customs of modern Sicilians because different experiences and different ways of understanding existence and the relationship between the divine and nature have fused to give life to a single culture that differs from all those that contributed to it. Although we often do not give the respect due to what is dissimilar, this culture is founded on differences – ones sometimes even extraordinary. And the greatest marvel to the strict and rational travelers who "explored" Sicily in the late 18th and early 19th centuries was the lack of conflict that existed between local tastes, languages and traditions. I think it is important to analyze the writings of such travelers – ten Frenchmen, six Germans, six Britons, two Danes, one Swiss, one Pole and one Russian – in their descriptions of a Sicily past but ready to re-emerge before our eyes as if two hundred years had passed in the twinkling of an eye. It is important because, as Vincenzo Consolo points out, these people "gave visibility to what, for Sciascia, previously was invisible to Sicilians."

The sensitivity of these travelers first made them hostile to and critical of the great confusion of styles and ruins that reigned on this island of wars and earthquakes. "Who can look without sorrow at these corpses of cities, these tombs of peoples?," wrote the son of the philosopher Jacobi who accompanied Stolberg in Sicily. Then they began to understand the sense of the contrasts when they reached Etna, the metaphor of the Sicilian microcosm, that breaks its apparent eternal quiet to liberate its pent-up energy with violence. The volcano destroys with its lava but turns fields into gardens with its black sand. It is a mountain that is paradise on the exterior but hell inside on which "the most delicate vegetation grows on blocks of spent fire," noted the German Johann Heinrich Bartels. It is Sicily's luxuriant growth that brings everything back to life. Another illuminating visit for the travelers was to the stone quarries of Syracuse, defined by Jacobi as "adventurous upsetting forms that bring to mind visions of an uncontrolled imagination." But in this place Bartels also saw how "the agile vine ties itself to the gigantic rock masses, between the fig trees and pomegranates that grow out of the stone," and the Frenchman Jean-Marie Roland de la Platière saw how the water had "formed a prodigious quantity of earthy stalactites that resemble petrified tree roots." Vivant Denon emphasized that what struck him about the place was "the contrast between the delicate and the terrible." This contrast has been the model for Sicilian taste, which Bartels defined as "extraordinary and marvellous," and which is extolled in the "Villa of the Monsters" in Bagheria. Previously Goethe had not hidden his disapproval in Palermo where the buildings rose "at random and at whim" and where a prince had built a bizarre palazzo just outside the city with sculptures of monsters. Almost without exception the travelers considered, this fascinating castle reprehensible and blasphemous. The disquiet that the Villa of the Monsters raised in these great minds and the space that they dedicated to it in their journals are symptomatic: unconsciously, they felt they had come across the root of a fundamental aspect of "Sicilianness." And it was Goethe who, with great intuition, created a neologism when he defined any manifestation of the Sicilian imagination as "Palagonian." Today we have only a

vague idea of what the villa looked like as, after the death of the prince, his brother-in-law destroyed many of the "monsters," sculptures and ornaments that, the Briton Patrick Brydone and the Pole Borch recorded, so struck the imagination of pregnant women scared of bringing a monster into the world. Two drawings by Count Borch survive that show the balustrade covered with chimerae, demons and creatures part human, part animal.

One of the drawings shows a woman with the head of a horse playing cards with a gryphon dressed as a horseman. There were also hydras, monkeys playing music, emperors with two noses or the body of a dwarf, statues with clocks in that moved their eyes, wrinkled babies, busts of women devoured by insects, deforming mirrors, columns of tools stuck together and chandeliers made from pieces of broken bottles and glasses. A sort of "red thread" links Etna, the Alcantara gorges, the "Turkish Steps" at Realmonte, the stone quarries of Syracuse, the Santoni of Palazzolo Acreide, the Fort at Gagliano Castelferrato, the Baroque corbels of Palazzo Villadorata in Noto, the monumental cemetery at Caltagirone, the Villa of the Monsters and another bewitched castle, built at Sciacca in the early 1900s by Don Filippo Bentivegna known as Filippu di li testi (Filippo of the heads). And a "red thread" also clearly emerges at any large

popular Sicilian festival: Santa Rosalia in Palermo, Sant'Agata in Catania or Sant'Alfio in Trecastagni. All are manifestations which express the ability of Sicilians to transform a stall into a palace, a bandstand into a princely castle or a cart into a firmament of stars, even with little or few means. These festivals show the desire of the Sicilian people to express themselves through elaborate architecture or decorations whether made from marble or cardboard. Also because, given the violence of the earthquakes that strike this island, no one knows which material might be the more resistant at the time. And while on the subject of festivals, as in many American and Australian cities these are perpetuated in miniature by the Sicilians who live there, it is worthwhile to discuss another fact that will help complete this fundamental portrait of the island and its inhabitants: what it is that has made Sicily expand beyond its confines through emigration. Giuseppe Tomaso di Lampedusa, author of the novel The Leopard, recalls how the islanders considered themselves to be the "salt of the earth" and, in part, they have been and are. It is as if the children of all those peoples who over the millennia have landed on the ship moored in the Mediterranean and contaminated by poverty had decided to disembark; not just in their countries of origin but also in new and distant lands, taking with them their

pride, the skills of their hands and minds and a
cardboard suitcase filled with olive oil, wine and
bread, the simplest expressions of a culture thousands
of years old. It is clear that Sicily cannot be considered
simply an island. It is a continent in miniature, a
melting pot of races, cultures, languages and religions.
For this reason experiments of great importance have
been carried out here over the centuries in the fields of
democracy and civil coexistence. The first was by
Roger de Hauteville in the year 1000 AD, which left
the defeated Arabs in charge of administration of the
bureaucracy and so created the first multi-racial
society in the world in which Catholics, Orthodox
Christians, Moslems and Jews lived peacefully
together, divided only by the color of their skins and
their houses: white, yellow, blue and pale pink. These
colors have survived in the smallest coastal and inland
villages, handed down by tradition though the colors
themselves have long lost their original significance.

Other examples also show how Sicily has been at
the forefront socially and politically: the first island
parliament, the plaques describing citizens' rights in
Sciacca in the 18th century, the socialist municipalism
of Giuseppe De Felice in 19th century Catania and the
Catholic municipalism of Don Sturzo in Caltagirone
in the 20th century. In addition, over the centuries
models of production were drawn up that may have
been unsophisticated but were respectful of the
environment; a learned culture was formed that
ranged from Giulio d'Alcamo to Pirandello, Sciascia,
Bufalino and a popular culture raised on a taste for
beauty that did not preclude any types of style and
which found its maximum expression via architectural
craftsmen.

When the backwardness of Sicily is discussed, what
is not taken into consideration is that the island is an
enormous laboratory which the world can watch to
understand the development of certain phenomena,
such as the Mafia. It is in Sicily that, in the age of the
global village, the whole world can discover – ways to
free itself from such monsters – which already are
beginning to run free in the rest of Italy and the
world. And, again, it is from this island at the center
of the Old World that a universal lesson might be
learned of civil coexistence and peace under the flag of
four colors: white, yellow, blue and pink.

452 top Bagheria: Villa of
the Monsters.

452-453 View of Noto.

453 top Noto: Palazzo
Ducezio.

454-455 Madonie: the Targa
Florio road race.

456-457 Cultivated land in
Sicily's interior.

CITIES, THE MARKS OF MAN

459 Detail of the Temple of Juno, at Agrigento, built between 460 and 440 BC on the top of a hill. Note the typical coloring of the columns made from sandstone and shell tufa.

icilian cities leave their mark, either forcing you to love them wildly or to hate them – there are no half measures. They require long descriptions, like memories of a trip to an exotic island, to provide an exact idea of them. Many are now dead although they once played a great part in the development of civilization: Imera, Eloro, Solunto, Megara, Morgantina, Naxos, Gela, Adranon, Segesta, Selinunte, ancient Noto and a thousand others, with temples, theaters, castles, houses, wells, roads and fortifications that recount a section of Sicilian history, just as those that are still alive embrace the traces of the past. It happens at Agrigento, where, in the words of Pirandello who was born there, the hill-top city is surrounded by "a landscape of Saracen olive trees that faces the edges of a plateau of blue clay on the African sea" and overlooks the Valley of the Temples, dressed with almond trees. On summer nights the valley becomes a single temple: the visitor sits in religious silence beneath the immense sky sprinkled with stars, enjoying the psalmodizing of the crickets and the smells of the plants wafted by the sea breeze, and caresses the columns made from shell tufa to understand the secret that transforms them at each sunrise into pure gold. It happens at Syracuse, built from blindingly white stone. Living stone, like that of Euralio Castle and the legendary walls of Dennis that were raised in twenty days by sixty thousand men and twelve thousand oxen, endorsements of the immense strength of the peoples that built these colossal monuments. Like the Greek theater, one of the largest in the world, where ancient Greek tragedies that demonstrate the immutability of man's feelings are re-enacted. This is also the city of cut rock, of the Ear of Dionysius with its worrying echoes, and of the Cave of the Rope-makers. And of course of the magnificent marbles in the Archaeological Museum, like the Landolina Venus and other masterpieces.

But there is also the Syracuse of the cathedral, which promises you respite from the heat and then traps you with its beauties, of the island of the Ortygia on spring afternoons that evoke legends like that of the nymph Arethusa who was turned into the spring of the Ciane river, where papyrus grows naturally. Then there is the papyrus itself, reduced to archaic and arcane paper by the Naro sisters,

custodians of the mysteries of their ancestor Landolina. And then there is Palermo, all blood and emotion, regal and popular, with its open dialect and picturesque phraseology. "Pani schittu e Cassaru" is used to describe the purebred Palermitan – he who has drunk water from the ancient spring of the Garaffo river – ready to renounce everything just to "ammulari i balati," i.e., wear down the wide paving slabs in the Corso (the Corso is called the Cassaro because there was once an Arab castle there). If during the evening stroll (inevitably called the cassariata) one passes a woman showing more than she should, she may be spoken of as "una di chiddi di lu Chianu di la Curti," referring to the statues of the naked women adorning the fountain in Pretoria Square, once known as Piano della Corte. This enormous 16th-century fountain also contains statues of men whom the Messinesi disfigured by hacking off their noses. As the punishment at the time for pimps was having one's nose cut, the Messinesi considered the comparison a good one. But the poor girl above might also be as ugly as "La Morti di lu Spitali," (the dead in the hospital) which refers to a 15th-century fresco painted during a restoration of Palazzo Sclafani, which was later transformed into a hospital. A quarrel is compared to the "Curtigghiu di li Raunisi" (courtyard of the Aragonese), where the commoners were always ready to "far sciarra" (argue) with the sellers. Yelling is also called vucciria, not for the assonance with the Italian verb "vociare" but for the name of the main market in Palermo, the vucci which means butchers.

A tall passerby is referred to as "autu quantu la culonna di Sannuminicu" (tall as the column of San Domenico), which was put up in the square of the church of San Domenico in 1726 to support the bronze statue of the Virgin Mary. Particularly lively children are compared, with an exaggerated anger, to "Diavuli di la Zisa" which refers to a 13th-century castle built in Arabic-Norman style in the Palermitan quarter of Zesa which depicts a great confusion of putti on the ceiling of the arched vault; the confusion is so great that, legend says, it is impossible to count them and they are considered little devils.

And when one loses one's patience – according to the folklorist Giuseppe Pitré who collected more than 14,000 proverbs, mottoes and phrases at the beginning

of the century – a rather indecent phrase describes one as "avilli quantu la cubbula di San Giulianu" ("having balls as big as the dome of San Giuliano" where size is an indication of the extent of one's anger). The huge dome only exists in the memory of the Palermitan people as it was destroyed to make room for the Teatro Massimo.

In Catania, the Cassaro is the Via Etnea which "is the incarnation of the very tip of vanity, like an honorary citizenship," wrote Riccardo Bacchelli. It is miles long and painted in bright colors by Antonio Aniante: "… it is the most famous ice-cream factory in the world and it is only authentic in summer: when the stars in the Catania sky are the largest and brightest in the firmament and the jasmine flowers that climb over the soft drink stalls are as large and plump as a child's hand." The old city center surrounds the Via Etnea with the Via dei Crociferi which, remembers Carlo Levi, "has a mysterious charm at night, with its churches and the arch, even if the headless horse no longer wanders around as it used to during the nights of the 18th century." Then there is the Castello Ursino which "looks at the sea from which the lava has separated it, the great face of the unfinished Benedictine black tower blacker than a black sky." The narrow perimeter of the Baroque city center built after the terrible earthquake of 1693 contains many other remarkable things, like the Cathedral, built over the remains of the Achillean Baths and in front of the statue of the elephant, symbol of the city, carved from lava. The elephant is nicknamed "liotru" which is a corruption of the name of the mythical magician Heliodorus. Close by there is a fountain of an underground river, the Amenano, which stands in the colorful setting of the fish market, then there is a Greek theater, an Odeon, the house-cum-museum of Giovanni Verga and another of Vincenzo Bellini, the theater dedicated to the composer, the University and the palazzo that belonged to the Prince of Biscari. Finally there is the Bellini Garden which Jules Verne described as "one of the most beautiful in Europe with … in the background, the superb volcano adorned with vapor."

In Messina, the background is the Calabrian coast because this city, destroyed by apocalyptic earthquakes in 1783 and 1908, is now characterized by low buildings. It was as if the port peninsula, known as St. Rainier's Scythe because of its shape, had rained blows down on the city to mow down victims of blood and stone. But the inhabitants of the city did not give in and in 1933, next to the Norman cathedral, built a bell-tower with the largest mechanical clock in the world, a symbol of their will. The clock is decorated with moving figures that represent historical and religious episodes. One of the figures is Death with scythe in hand which is intended to be both a warning and a commemoration of a resistance that is only for

the strong. In order to comply with anti-seismic regulations during reconstruction after the last disaster, the new buildings had to be built low, and so that they might still have some exceptional feature to boast, the unknown craftsmen put all their efforts into the decorations with a taste that was fully "palagonian." In search of their lost architectural heritage, they first modelled columns, capitals, balustrades, corbels, fascias, panels, caryatids, gargoyles, flowers, fruit, dragons, putti, centaurs, chimerae, and every sort of monstrous animal using

clay and chalk. They made moulds filled with cement and marble dust that were sacrificed with blows of a hammer when the decoration was finished.

Ragusa and her twin city Ibla were also born as the result of an earthquake and are the daughters of an ancient urban center. The two grew clinging onto the sides of contiguous hills joined by a series of steps and bridges, "wearing their Baroque with the reserve of an old lady," wrote Gesualdo Bufalino, who went on to say that, to visit Ibla, "a certain quality of spirit is required … one professes a passion for architectural machinations where the fondness for airborne form hides, until the last, the coup de thèatre of the false perspective." This is the case with the masterpiece of Rosario Gagliardi, the master carpenter turned architect extraordinaire: Ibla cathedral, dedicated to St. George, represents a sort of "summa" of religious architecture in Sicily up till the end of the 18th century. At the top of a long flight of steps, its imposing facade appears ringed by a railing of iron lacework. The facade is so beautiful that it was nearly copied in a reconstruction of the nearby 16th-century church of San Giuseppe. Then there is the Ragusan version of Palagonian style with the grotesque figures and gargoyles on the Zacco, Consentini and Lupis palazzi which seem to represent figures from popular fables.

Standing on Frederick Swabian tower in the regal town of Enna, it is easy to understand why the Arabs thought of dividing up the island into three valleys. Enna is at the center of the island of three headlands and at times she hides herself from them in a veil of fog, just like a grand lady. Enna is the city where men do not feel the need to fly like birds because from here it seems possible to reach out and touch Etna. Enna is almost unassailable, like the Lombard Castle, having been built on a mountain from which parts of the slopes were cut away to prevent scaling, and the character of the inhabitants is the same - kind but distant - until their mouths open in a fraternal and winning smile signaling eternal friendship. It is a real treasure, like the one inside the cathedral with its rather shabby exterior: extraordinary pointed arches on basalt columns and a caisson ceiling of moving beauty and splendid fonts. There is another treasure chest with its precious jewels: the museum dedicated to Alessi that contains Sicily's religious masterpieces of the goldsmith's art. Confronted by the "Crown of the Madonna," the spectator is breathless with admiration. The Montalbano brothers from Palermo dedicated an entire year of work to create this perfect example of the prodigiousness of the Sicilians.

Caltanissetta, on the other hand, is a mixture of the smells of sulfur and ploughed fields. It has a museum dedicated to the sulfur mines that represented both the daily bread and the suffering of youngsters little more than children, who were painted by Onofrio Tomaselli breathless from the effort of transporting their loads of yellow rock in the palpable heat. They are so lifelike that you feel you could ask them about their red-haired companion, Ciaula. Caltanissetta is so obsessed with water that it built a 16th-century fountain with a bronze triton and seahorse right in front of the cathedral.

This too is a Palagonian city to judge by the large anthropomorphic and zoomorphic corbels of the palace built by Count Luigi Moncada e Aragona in the 17th century. It is also small, poor and often forgotten though one of Sicily's best cultural lodes is to be found

462-463 The Concordia Temple (6th century BC) seems almost whole despite the fragility of the shell tufa. It is the best conserved Greek temple after the Temple of Theseus in Athens (made from marble). Experts believe that its survival is due to the fact that it was transformed into a three-nave Christian church by Gregory, the bishop of Agrigento.

463 top left The Temple of the Dioscuri was built during the 5th century BC and gravely damaged when the city was destroyed by the Carthaginians. It was restored in later centuries.

463 top right This is what remains of the Temple of Hercules, the oldest in Agrigento. It once had thirty-eight columns and was adorned with statues, wall linings and paintings.

464 top *The hexastyle Temple E at Selinunte dates from the 5th century BC.*

464-465 *Temple C at Selinunte was constructed during the first half of the 5th century BC.*

here, hidden behind its fortifications like the Pietrarossa castle that dominates the city.

And finally there is Trapani, the Trapani of the wind, the salt-mines, nautical beams, tuna-fishing and couscous. It is also the city of the Odyssey because it seems that Homer was born here – not in Greece – and he wasn't a man, but a woman, so much so that her apprehension of the sea is made quite transparent in her work. Bradford and Butler and then Pococka have tried to rediscover the places along this coast where Odysseus lived his adventures. Trapani also has

an Arab quarter around the port in which the principal roads are shari, the secondary roads are darb, and the alleyways and courtyards are azzicca. In the nearby quarter of Giudecca, the Spedaletto and the nearby tower were built with diamond-pointed ashlars. The Santuario dell'Annunziata (Sanctuary of the Annunciation) has a splendid rose window and a Gothic portal and, inside, there is the Cappella dei Marinai (Sailors' Chapel) and the statue of the "Madonna of Trapani" that stands over a silver model of the city. Near to the Sanctuary and its imposing Baroque bell-tower stands the monastery of the Annunciation that houses the museum with its "magnificent grand staircase." The museum contains a late-18th-century scene of the birth of Christ made entirely from coral which unites two of the city's traditional arts – the carving of coral and crib scenes – toru and sangu.

These cities that have been discussed are the provincial capitals but there are so many more extraordinary towns, for example, Taormina, the pearl that clings to the flanks of Mount Tauro with a splendid panorama over the sea and Etna, a glorious Greco-Roman amphitheater, the cathedral, and the Corvaja and Ciampoli palaces.

There is also the medieval Erice, built inside a triangle - a foggy town that has been sacred to women for millennia and is now dedicated to science - and the Palagonian Noto, really just a large theater where the song of life is sung. Caltagirone, famous for pottery and its 142-step stairway; Monreale with its Norman cathedral and cloister with 228 decorated columns; Cefalù with another Norman cathedral and the Portrait of an Unknown Man by Antonello da Messina; Tindari, with its Greek theater that opens onto the sea and salt-water lakes that continually change shape, and from where one can see Lipari, with the Norman cathedral that was transformed into a Baroque building and the castle that was converted into a museum of Aeolian civilization are more examples.

Then we have Acireale and Sciacca, spa cities rich with tradition; Marsala with its sweet wine, the gate built to celebrate the arrival of Garibaldi's troops, and the Phoenician island of Mozia. And then Piazza Armerina with its mosaics and the Norman Palio. And Modica, Scicli, Palazzolo del Barocco, Gagliano del Castello Ferrato, Mazara del Vallo, the hexagonal Grammichele, Sambuca-Zamut, Santo Stefano of the majolica tiles, Savoca of the mummies, Sortino with its honey and Maniace which remained under its feudal regime until just a few years ago. And the newest of all, Gibellina, another creation following an earthquake, the most recent in 1968. This list could go on and on. It makes one understand the reserve of the emigré who prefers to hold inside him that which he would like everyone to share.

THE PALERMO
OF THE CASSARO

466 top A bronze quadriga by Mario Rutelli adorns the top of the Politeama Garibaldi, designed by Damiani Almeyda during the 19th century.

466-467 The church of San Giovanni degli Eremiti was built during the Norman period by Islamic workers.

467 top View of Palermo with Monte Pellegrino behind.

467 bottom The Teatro Massimo was built between 1875 and 1897 by architects Giovan Battista and Ernesto Basile, father and son. Many buildings were pulled down to make way for it, including the church of San Giuliano with its massive dome.

468-469 The fountain of Piazza Pretoria was commissioned from Francesco Camilliani by Don Pietro di Toledo for his Florentine villa. It was purchased in 1578 by the Palermo Senate and placed in the popularly named "Chianu di la Curti."

470 and 471 The Vucciria is the best known of Palermo's outdoor markets. It was depicted in several splendid paintings by Renato Guttuso and takes its name from the vucci (butchers) because it used to be the city's main meat market. Another market, which no longer exists, is remembered in

*Palermitan idioms, the
Curtigghiu di li Raunisi
(courtyard of the Aragonese),
in which tough commoners
fought with sellers to obtain
lower prices. U curtigghiu di
li Raunisi is also the title of an
anonymous farce and the first
example of popular Sicilian
theater before the Mafiusi
di la Vicaria, by Rizzotto.*

CATANIA
BLACK
WITH LAVA

472-473 The Bellini Garden is the largest green area in the city. It has trees, such as gigantic ficus, that are hundreds of years old, and various ducks and swans. There also used to be monkeys and even two elephants (the symbol of the city is an elephant called liotru made of black lava).

The first elephant, Menelik, was a gift to the city from King Umberto I of Italy in 1890 who had earlier received it from the ruler of Ethiopia, Menelik II. The animal is now stuffed and kept in the University Museum. The second, Tony, was given to the city by the Darix Togni circus in 1965.

473 top The statue of
Ferdinand I Bourbon is
by Antonio Calì. It was
decapitated shortly after the
arrival of Garibaldi's troops.
The gallery of Palazzo Biscari
can be seen behind; it faces
onto Catania marina.

473 center View of the
Baroque Benedictine
monastery, rebuilt after
the 1693 earthquake.

473 bottom Detail of the
ornamental decorations of
the facade of Palazzo Biscari,
designed by Francesco
Battaglia.

474-475 The domes of two
Baroque Catanese churches:
the snowy peak of Etna forms
the backdrop.

THE WHITE CITY
OF SYRACUSE

476 Syracuse was founded in the second half of the 8th century BC by Corinthian colonists. Its continuous political and cultural influence culminated during the dynasty of the Dinomenids. During the reign of Hiero I the Syracuse court was visited by the most famous poets of the era, such as Simonides, Bacchylides, Pindar and Aeschylus. It reached the peak of its political power during the tyranny of Dionysius (between 406 and 367 BC) and then decline set in, marked by internal struggles, pressure from enemies and heavy foreign domination, the last being that of the Bourbons. It became part of the kingdom of Italy after Garibaldi captured Sicily and Naples with his 1000 "Redshirts." The picture shows moorings for fishing boats on the Nazario Sauro Riviera inside the city's smaller harbor.

477 The Greek theater, surrounded by stone quarries, is one of the largest and most perfect from antiquity. It was made from white stone by the architect Demekopos (also known as "Myrilla" – meaning unguent – as this was what was distributed to the public during its inauguration). Syracuse was where Epicharmus, the father of Greek comedy, lived. Along with Athens and Alexandria, Syracuse was one of the major centers of theatrical culture. It is said that Syracuse was where Aeschylus' tragedy The Persians was first shown. Aeschylus was also the author of The Etneans,which was written to commemorate the foundation of Etna by Hiero I and which first was performed in Syracuse in 476 BC.

MESSINA, DAUGHTER OF AN EARTHQUAKE

478-479 *Detail of the 16th-century fountain of Orion executed by Giovanni Montorsoli and Domenico Vanello, built to commemorate the construction of the city's first aqueduct. The fountain is one of the few ancient monuments to have survived the series of earthquakes that has hit the city over the centuries.*

478 left *This is an aerial view of Punta Faro, the tip of land that sticks out into the fish-filled waters of the Mediterranean towards mainland Italy.*

479 top View of the city center. The city was completely destroyed in 1908 by a violent earthquake. It was rebuilt in keeping with anti-seismic criteria but suffered further damage from heavy bombing during World War II.

CALTANISSETTA
CAPITAL
OF SULPHUR

480 Caltanissetta was once the capital of the Sicilian sulfur industry, to which it has dedicated a museum. The world of those working in the sulfur mines was described in *Ciaula Discovers the Moon*, a novella by Luigi Pirandello. The city is dominated by the ancient castle of Pietrarossa, built as an Arab fortification and captured by the Norman count, Roger de Hauteville, in 1086. After chasing out the Saracens for good, Roger founded the Priory of San Giovanni, around which the city grew up.

REGAL ENNA

481 Enna is the highest provincial capital in Europe. All of Sicily lies at its feet. It was from here that the Arab conquerors decided to divide Sicily into three political territories: the valley of Maraza, the valley of Demone, and the valley of Noto. Until 1927 the city was called Castrogiovanni, the Italian corruption of the Arab name Qasr Yannah which, in turn, was how the Saracens transcribed the Latin name of Castrum Hennae.

THE MOSAICS OF PIAZZA ARMERINA

484-485 *Charming image of Piazza Armerina against a gloomy, stormy background. The city is also known for the Palio dei Normanni (Norman horse race) that takes place on August 15th. It celebrates the festival of the Madonna delle Vittorie (Virgin of the Victories), whose standard was given to the inhabitants of the town by Count Roger for their contribution in expelling the Saracens.*

482 and 483 This is a series of photographs of the Roman Villa del Casale, in Piazza Armerina in the province of Enna. A series of excavations begun in 1929 by Paolo Orsi has uncovered several superb mosaics. The mosaics in living rooms, galleries, peristyles, courtyards and hot bath rooms on different levels of a slope are protected by plastic covers. Their beauty and the huge area they cover make Villa del Casale a unique monument.

BAROQUE IBLA

486-487 Ibla was rebuilt in the Baroque style in 1730 after being destroyed in the 1693 earthquake. The picture shows the oldest section of the town where traces of prehistoric settlements have been found. Ibla stands in front of a hill where Ragusa is built, to which it is joined by a series of steps and bridges. The two districts used to be autonomous – Ibla was home to the ancient feudal nobility and Ragusa to the emerging economic classes – but they were unified in 1926 and a year later became the capital of the province.

TAORMINA
THE PEARL

488 This fine aerial view of Taormina with its Greco-Roman theater demonstrates how the city deserves its description as the "Pearl of the Ionian Sea." Taormina's theater is the second largest classical theater in Sicily. It was built by the Greeks on the top of a hill and was later enlarged and almost completely rebuilt by the Romans.

488-489 The Gulf of Naxos and Etna are the natural background to the ancient theater which the Romans turned into an amphitheater for gladiatorial fights. The remains of a small temple were found on the eastern side of the cavea.

489 top Taormina's attractive public gardens.

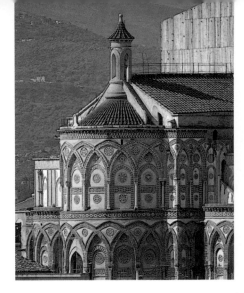

MOSAICS
ON THE COLUMNS

490 and 491 The cathedral of Monreale, built between 1172 and 1189, is a real work of Norman art. The interior of the three-nave basilica is decorated with Byzantine style mosaics, in particular the central apse with its splendid image of Christ Pantocrator. The cloister square dates from the 12th century; the pointed arches are supported by 228 twin columns, both decorated with mosaics or sculpted.

TRAPANI
AND THE SEA

492-493 *The warm light of sunset veils the city of Trapani against the background of the Egadian islands. The city's maritime tradition is reflected in the Cappella dei Marinai (Sailors'* *Chapel) in the Santuario dell'Annunziata (Sanctuary of the Annunciation) and in the delicious dishes of steamed couscous served with an infinite variety of fish condiments.*

THE NORMAN CITY OF CEFALU

494-495 *Cefalù gets its name from a rock in the shape of a head that stands over the town. It was founded by the Greeks and became an independent diocese under the Normans. Roger II built many buildings and* *churches, including the Norman cathedral, one of Sicily's most beautiful. The excellent painting Portrait of an Unknown Man, by Antonello da Messina, hangs in the Mandralisca Museum in Cefalù.*

THE SEA OF COLA PESCE

For those who were born in Sicily, going back is like returning to the maternal womb, protected from all outside interference, in an atmosphere made torpid by the humid warmth, where time passes slowly, measured by the comforting echo of a heartbeat. The island is a microcosm marked by incredibly rapid and violent vital processes, but it is also mysterious and ineluctable, where one is separated from reality and surrounded by an enormous mass of amniotic fluid. The fluid is the sea and the song of the surf is the sound of the mother's heartbeat; and as their rhythm is the indication of her mood, so the sea is both loved and hated. Its colors are simply enchanting: white with foam at Sciacca, violet at Trezza, dark blue in front of Palermo, lightest green at Brucoli, phosphorescent at Zingaro, and red where the sea-birds make their home in the marsh at Vindicari.

The sea to Sicilians is the gateway to the world but also from where invaders, merchants and pirates arrived. The coast is dotted with the ruins of look-out towers for the "Mammatraj," the terrible Turkish pirates named after the most ferocious, Mohammed Dragut. The memory of these pirates is so great that down the centuries even to the present day, Sicilian mothers frighten their restless children by telling them, "Look out, here comes the Mammatraju."

It was as a result of this fear that villages and towns began to be built inland on the hills out of sight of the sea, but on all the small islands that surround Sicily there were towns and cities where it was impossible to hide, whose histories are even more closely linked to the sea.

First, there are the Aeolian islands which one can reach at night using the volcano as a lighthouse. It used to guide sailors from far-off places who went there to purchase obsidian, the black and shiny volcanic glass that was used to make knives and arrow points and axe heads before iron was known. The ancient Mediterranean civilization was actually called an "obsidian civilization" and the Aeolian islands were at its center. The most isolated is Alicudi, a lump of rock covered with heather and flailed by the wind. It is surrounded by deep blue water that used to be watched with apprehension from the timpuni de' fimmini, the shelter where the women fled when pirate ships were sighted.

Then there is Stromboli, with its black beach named Ficogrande, the Sciara del fuoco and Ginostra, bedecked with helichrysum and its satellite, Strombolicchio, which looks like a petrified ship with a figurehead in the shape of the head of an animal.

Vulcano is the island of medicinal herbs and of Venus' Pool; Salina was seen by the ancients as a woman sleeping among the waves who guards gigantic ferns, fields of camomile, thousand-year-old chestnut trees and Perciati of curdled lava in her bosom. Filicudi is ringed by coral, has a prehistoric village that faces the warm southern wind and is known for its remarkable cliff named the Scoglio della Canna. The waters of Panarea are warmed by underwater geysers that look like the mouths of Hell. Offshore lie the four islets of Dattilo, Liscabianca, Liscanera and Basiliuzzo; the latter is home to jackdaws and seagulls and used to see the seasonal herding of the island's animal flocks.

Finally, there is Lipari, the kingdom of Liparo who left his crown to Aeolus, the husband of his daughter, to return to the continent. Lipari has white beaches, salt-works, a castle that stands on vitreous rock, and flows of obsidian and pumice stone. Lipari is also the island of Malvasia wine and the Dionysian cult of the theater for which a huge number of votive masks inspired by dramatic characters made from colored terracotta have been found by archaeologists. Lipari is always visible from the tops of the high mastheads on the boats of the swordfish fisherman in the Strait of Messina.The lookouts scrutinize the water for hours until they see the froth which indicates the courting dance of the fish when they pass in this area.

Once sighted, the signal is given to harpoon them using the dreffinere (a special kind of harpoon) with long cables, then the fish are allowed to tire themselves out as they pull the boat, and the crew try to stick them before pulling them aboard. The swordfish hunt is relived in June each year for San Giovanni in a pantomime played out among the cliffs of Acitrezza. This is an ancient ritual that follows the dictates of popular magic in which the fishermen try in vain to catch their prey – the role of the fish is given to the most handsome and strongest boy in the village – but the fish does not just escape, he ends up tipping the boat over.

It is curious to know that a similar ceremonial pantomime is performed by aboriginal Australians, but this is no more than a sign that man is the same in the most arcane and intimate expression of his feelings all over the world.

The Pelagian islands are more greatly marked by their nearest continental neighbor, Africa, which has bequeathed them bronze-colored coleoptera, unwinged grasshoppers and strange lizards. In summer, sea turtles lay their eggs on these, the southernmost islands in Europe, and regina falcons arrive from Madagascar, so called because they were protected by edict by Queen Eleonora d'Arborea centuries ago. The smallest of the Pelagian islands is Lampione, then there is Linosa with its extinct volcanoes and the choral singing of the shearwaters and the yellow crickets. Lampedusa was once Phoenician and later Roman. Its thick forests were filled with foxes, boar and small deer until 1839 when it was sold by the Tomasi princes to Ferdinand II. He sent 120 colonists who were given rights to "free hunting and fishing" in addition to the possibility of using the trees; this led to the desertification of the island in just a few decades and to the transformation of its beauty into African landscapes, some of which are breathtakingly beautiful like the Isola dei Conigli, with its very light blue sea. Part African and part European, a pact was signed in 1221 for it to be administered jointly by Frederick II and the Emir of Tunis, Abbuissac, as well as its sister island Bent el rion (Arabic for daughter of the wind), which has been transformed into Pantelleria in Italian. The island boasts the Sesi, a group of magical megaliths created five thousand years ago by ancient inhabitants of the island, its dammusi (cool, ancient cubic houses), the Barbacane castle made from black lava, Venus' Mirror (a warm lake inside a crater), and the Point in the shape of an elephant's head drinking from the sea, with the ears flapping. When the flowers of the caper plants open to resemble wild orchids, the island is a real spectacle.

On the maps Ustica looks like a tiny round lentil like those cultivated by the farmers on its bare volcanic slopes. The name "Mount of the Turkish Guard" speaks volumes about the massacres of the Lipari colonists on Ustica and the island, after a long period spent housing a prison, has now been recognized as a

chest of treasures: its fauna and flora and iridescent coastal caves have been protected in a marine reserve.

Lastly, there are the Egadi islands.

Marettimo has great pink stone cliffs and immense caves with high-flown names; little Levanzo has cave drawings over ten thousand years old that show tuna fishing as it is still practiced on Favignana, Odysseus' island of goats.

Favignana gets its name from the favonio, the wind that pushes these enormous, silent, silver fish into the nets. Favignana has always been linked to tuna fishing as can be seen by the splendid tuna processing plant built by Palermo architect Damiani Almeyda using tufa extracted from the same island and famous throughout the Mediterranean for its softness. The fish are lifted in the boats after the occisa, an equal armed struggle between man and the enormous king of the sea: maneuvering ritenute and tradimenti (ropes), the crew lift the heavy nets from the water to the sound of the cialome, the characteristic songs of the tuna fishermen:

Aya mola aya mola
Gesù Cristu ccu' li santi
Aya mola aya mola
E lu santu Sarvaturi
Aya mola aya mola

The net of the death chamber, the last of the process, fills like an enormous sack inside the square formed by the boats.

Gnanzou
San Cristofuru
Gnanzou
Granni e Grossu
Gnanzou

The net tightens as the water drains out.

Isa isa
Zza' Monica 'n cammisa
SPARA A TUNNINAAA!

The tails of the tuna flail wildly like scythes, sending spray everywhere as the fish gasp for life. Then the crew guide these enormous fish with hooks on the tip of long poles towards the crocc'a 'mmenzu who pull them inside the black barges, dodging to avoid the lethal blows of the tails.

The occisa takes place in an unreal atmosphere in which the participants are baptized by blood and salt water as though taking part in a cathartic pagan rite in which one is struck by the absence of the sacrificial victims' screams of agony. If the tuna could scream, tuna killing would have never taken place. Instead, the tuna fish business was perhaps Sicily's largest industry until the 19th century. There were twenty-one plants that treated the "sea pig" (it was called this because every part of it was used) in which the fish were cooked in enormous caldrons so that their meat could be tinned with olive oil.

498 The Turkish Steps in Realmonte in the province of Agrigento. This unusual cliff sculpted by the sea was connected in popular imagination with the raids carried out by Saracen pirates during the 15th and 16th centuries.

The tins were differently colored depending on which part of the fish was used: the soft belly, the dorsal zone (tuna proper), or the flanks and the tail. The same tuna fishermen were responsible for decapitating and cleaning out the insides of the fish as well as extracting the ovarian sacs of the females, which were sun-dried to make botargo. The rest of the sea-pig was left to steep in the camposanto (in the center of the tuna boat) from which oil was made that was used in foundries; then the dried residue was either turned into a flour to be used for animal feed or into a fertilizer.

The Sicilian tuna boats were so important to the economy of the island that, during the tuna killing season, their owners and administrators could not be sent to prison. The "tuna-fish culture" also led to the construction of many lovely buildings, like the plants at Scopello and Marzamemi – the property of the Nicolaci di Villadorata family that lived in the palace with the corbels carved in the shape of lions, monsters, cherubs and pairs of winged horses.

The new factories were built to replace the plant at Bafuto that had become unhealthy due to the malaria in the nearby marshes of Vindicari. Then there is the plant at Capo Passero, painted in a picture held in the Museum of Naples, a beautiful building in the Spanish style belonging to the princes of Bruno di Belmonte but erected in the 18th century by the curiously named Palermo baron Rau Xa Xa. This building is surrounded by fishermen's houses and dwarf palm trees. It stands beside the ruins of a Greek tuna processing plant and what is known as the "Pantano Marghella," a large natural salt-pan, because tuna plants always needed large quantities of salt. The loveliest salt-works, now abandoned, are those at Vindicari and Marsala. They are home to a huge number of birds whose thousands of colors at sunrise and sunset testify to the magnificent variety of nature.

It was in Hector's Salt-works at Marsala, while the great blades of the windmills sang as they caught the wind and the last red rays of the sun were reflected in the large tanks in which the salt was "taking," that Don Turi Toscano, overseer of the salt-works, explained to me that one should not fear the sea. "Over there is Mozia which used to be Phoenician – there are still their tanks for preparing boats and drawings of panthers, but Garibaldi was there too. That's where they found a statue, I tell you, of Cola Pesce." Cola Pesce is the main character in an infinite series of Sicilian legends. He was an ordinary boy but so good at swimming that he became a sort of deity, half man and half fish. With sufficient courage to dive down to get the crown that the king had thrown into the deep on a whim, and with a heart as big as the sea, he decided to stay in the underwater world and reign over one of the three columns on which Sicily rests so that it would not collapse.

That is how he is portrayed in the statue dedicated to him in Catania, one of the most recent ones made in Sicily.

"After all this time down there," went on Don Turi, "Cola will by now have made friends with some large fish. And if I fall in the water, me that can't swim, he'll shout out: Do me a favor as I can't go, there's Don Turi, go and get him and take him up. That's why you shouldn't be afraid of the sea."

As you scan the horizon for ferocious pirates, the sea of Cola Pesce merges with the sky to become a single entity, allowing one's imagination to soar to far-off countries like the one where the Vuvitini live.

The Vuvitini are men just knee-high to a grasshopper; they inhabit the part of the world where we place the soles of our feet, and watch us from the sloughs of the salt-pans.

500-501 *The Arab name of Pantelleria, Bent el rion, means "daughter of the wind." Five thousand years ago, the island was inhabited by a people that built strange but lovely monuments today known as the Sesi. The island is also interesting for its thermal lake known as Venus' Mirror, which lies in an extinct volcano.*

501 bottom *Ustica used to suffer terribly from pirate raids; today it is a sort of capital of the sea thanks to the institution of the "Golden Trident" awards, a near equivalent of the "Oscars" in the scuba-diving world.*

THE SEVEN DAUGHTERS OF KING AEOLUS

502-503 The stacks and
the island of Vulcano,
seen from Lipari.
The Aeolian islands are
a true paradise of limpid
waters, luxuriant vegetation
and natural monuments.
The islands were at the center
of ancient Mediterranean
civilization because of their
abundance of obsidian,
a natural glass produced
during the final stages of a
volcanic eruption. The glass
was used to make tools,
knives, blades and small axes.

503 top A typical fishing
boat pulled up out of the
water on a beach in Salina.

503 center White fishermen's
houses stretch out along the
beach and slopes of the island
of Vulcano.

503 bottom The central
crater on Stromboli rises over
2953 feet above sea level.

504-505 The crater of
Vulcano dominates the
sea and islands below.

506-507 Salina was called
Dydime by the ancients and
was thought of as a woman
lying asleep in the waves.

507 top Panarea was
originally a volcanic island.
Remains of Neolithic and
Stone Age human
settlements have been
found here.

507 bottom Part of the
cultivated area on Salina
is used to grow capers.
The flower of the spiny
caper plant is similar
to a wild orchid.

THE SACRIFICE
OF THE KING
OF THE SEA

508 and 509 The pictures
show boats moored in the
harbor and fishermen
mending their nets on
Favignana. The ritual of
the mattanza (tuna killing)
is celebrated each year by
the island's fishermen, as
shown on the following
pages. It is similar in nature
to the contest between a
bull and a matador.

509

510, 511 and 512-513
The duel between the tuna fishermen and the giant silver fish with scythe-like tail is a sort of metaphor of life and death in which man and his prey meet equally armed. There is no cruelty during the blood-spattered spray of the occisa but a battle fought for the spirit of survival. The ritual is an ancient one as shown by the wall-paintings in the Genovese Cave in Levanzo, which date from 12,000 BC. The battle takes place when the fish return from the Atlantic to the Mediterranean to breed.

LINOSA, THE PAINTED ISLAND

514 and 515 On the left, colored houses on the island of Linosa, with giant terracotta pots of geraniums outside. On the right shows the lighthouse, with prickly pear plants in the foreground; these are one of the few plants that flourish on lava-based soil. Linosa is a volcanic island and even the walls that line the roads and paths are made from lava.

THE AFRICAN
PELAGIAN
ISLANDS

516, 517 and 518-519
*Lampedusa was covered by
forests that were home to
foxes, boar and small deer
until the mid-19th century,
when King Ferdinand II sent
120 colonists to the island.
In just a few decades they
turned the rerdant land*
*into a desert but
Lampedusa's African
landscapes are no less
lovely, like the view of
the Isola dei Conigli.
The sea around Lampedusa
is a turquoise blue and
turtles now return to the
beaches to lay their eggs.*

THE LAND OF
THE CAROB TREE

To me, the most authentic landscape in Sicily is the one that Piero Guccione painted of the infinite, uninterrupted background of sea and sky, as is appropriate to an island. Enzo Siciliano compared Guccione's pictures of the gullies of Ragusa to "a sorrowful melody with the carob trees in agony, worn away, the sadness of the stones at sundown and the glory of the corn-fields." It is a visible melody that can penetrate and educate the soul to the point, writes Bartels, that in Sicily "the last of the peasants has more feeling for beauty, truth and artistic expression than one of our orchestra conductor." Like Don Paolo from Sortino, who is one of the last craftsmen to carve wood into walking sticks, pipes and animal collars. Shepherds travel from a distance to allow him to choose the cianciane (bells) to attach to their animals' collars. Don Paolo's finely tuned ear enables him to select a small bell for each animal which harmonizes with those of the others in the herd so that the shepherd can recognize his herd by the melody it makes whenever it moves. Who knows which people over the millennia brought this custom with them for in Sicily nature too is an overlay of cultures. Almost all the plants chosen to be a symbol of the island have been imported: the vine, the olive, the almond and the pistachio by the Greeks, citrus fruits and the mulberry by the Arabs, and the aloe and the prickly pear by the Spanish after the discovery of America.

And it is surprising that among the cuiri alleri (bushes) of the broom on the slopes of Etna, a northern tree like the birch grows and that there is a Sicilian variant known as arvulu cruci cruci in the village of Polizzi Generosa. In this land of contrasts, we find African dwarf palms and the beech that grows on the slopes of the volcano and on the Madonie and Nebrodi hills. Every type of plant or tree that grows in Sicily has a close link with the religiousness, ceremonies, legends and medicines of the people. The Sicilian birch is shown with Jupiter on a coin of Etna; papyrus was used until the 18th century as an ornament for religious ceremonies; the old people of San Vito Lo Capo and Porto Palo plait baskets and elegant fans using the curina (heart) of the dwarf palm; and the whole of the almond tree is used – like the tuna and the pig – to create oils, essences, sweets, wood, charcoal slack and even a soft soap. Crossing the Sicilian landscape, the traveler is struck by the expanses of low, supported vines, florid in the land of Dionysus, used to

produce the white wines of Alcamo and Etna, the generous reds of the volcano, the Cerasuolo of Vittoria and dessert wines to accompany philosophizing or idle gossip, such as the Malvasia of Lipari, the muscats of Pantelleria, Noto and Syracuse, and Marsala that one can taste even with one's eyes. "Is this wine which smiles below the froth? Or carnelian topped by a row of pearls?," wrote the medieval Arab poet Hamdis when remembering the wine of Noto, his birthplace.

The presence of the green, orange and yellow citrus orchards on the slopes of Etna is announced by the perfume of the orange blossoms. The trees bring forth fruit that look like small suns able to brighten the greyest day or give blood and life back to a pale child.

The wheat is the child of the summer but is then changed into loaves so elaborate they look like lacework at the festival of San Giuseppe. The perfumed herb, basil, is another product of the heat and on June 24th is used to "sancire i comparaggi" (used to celebrate a special bond between the father and the godfather of a child) in enormous terracotta containers tied with a red ribbon. The sun also serves to dry the tomatoes that hang in great red bunches on the lime-coated walls of the houses in Trapani, and to bring the peppers and eggplants to the right size and maturity to make caponata, the bittersweet dish that is the gastronomic version of Palagonian taste. The green meadows, more numerous than one might think, are the grazing land for the musical flocks of Don Paolo. I remember him in a farmhouse with paralupi, a fig leaf in one hand and illuminated by a ray of sunshine that entered between some loose tiles, reciting prayers before a caldron for tuma, primosale, cannistrato and pecorino cheeses. He said three pateravegloria to the ricotta cheese, skimming it religiously with a terracotta cup, then baptized it with the nectar provided by the master honeymaker from Sortino, Don Giuseppe Blancato. Then there are the thousand-year-old Saracen olive trees that have seen and produced so much. People who abandon their fields always keep a few olive trees for themselves to make oil for their family's use; it is always unique in its taste and smell. But there are other extremely old trees, like the "Hundred Horse Chestnut" which got its name, it is said, when Queen Joanna of Aragon and her entire retinue took shelter there from a storm. Almost four thousand years old and 171 feet in circumference, the chestnut stands in Sant'Alfio and used to contain "a house in which there

was an oven for drying chestnuts, hazelnuts and almonds," according to Houel. Despite the public image that Sicily has of being a bare and barren land, it boasts 521 acres of oaks, cork, holm-oaks and chestnut trees on the Nebrodi, Madonie, Caronie, Iblei and Erei hills, and on Etna, in the ancient hunting grounds of the kings such as Ficuzza wood, and in the forest at Santo Pietro where for centuries the craftsmen of Caltagirone got the wood they used to heat the ovens to bake their pottery.

Sicily has another treasure up in the hills: water. The Simeto and Alcantara rivers have their sources in the same area and have worked at creating their own colossal Palagonian works of art over the millennia: extraordinary ravines carved out of ancient lava beds which, in the case of the Alcantara, drop dozens of feet between the waterfall and the rapids. As it washed away the rock, the river has formed fantastic figures which seem almost to come to life at sunset and dance to the sound of a pipe organ in a representation of primordial chaos. The Arabs used this fantastic river as a breeding ground for crocodiles, as they did in the Abbas (the Oreto) in the province of Palermo and in the Anapo around Syracuse. The latter has something else in common with Alcantara: towering over it is an immense and extraordinary rock. This is Pantalica, the sacred mountain of the Siculi tribe, that stands in the midst of gigantic plane and oleander trees. It is an immense open-air cathedral that has stood for millennia while the river murmurs its eternal prayer. Pantalica is also linked for me to the memory of an authentically regal gesture made by Prince Charles of Britain some years ago when the area was still in the charge of the Forestry Commission; wanting to pay homage to this magnificent monument, he cleared up some of the waste paper thoughtlessly left by tourists too obtuse to recognize the holiness of the spot. This was a reconciliatory gesture for how certain monarchs have treated nature in Sicily. It was the English ambassador, Lord Hamilton, who recorded in his journal after accompanying Ferdinand, the first king of the Two Sicilies, on a hunting trip, how in eight days in Ficuzza wood, the gentlemen of the court had killed "a thousand deer, a hundred boar, three wolves and so very many foxes." He emphasized how the hunt had been "a massacre and not true sport." It is hardly surprising that there is no longer any trace of these animals in Sicily, with the exception of the fox, and they are having to be reintroduced to certain wooded areas. One such place is the Zingaro, one of the loveliest nature reserves on the island and where Uzzo Cave is located. This is the cave that contained remains of men, deer, boar and bears that lived ten thousand years ago. There are 3954 hundred acres of wild and bare land, reached through the track of a road that was never completed. It used to be such a poverty stricken area that the people used to scrape the ash trees for something to keep them from starvation. Imagine a petrified white snow on a sea like an enormous jewel, beneath an African sky that hasn't seen the path of a golden eagle for twenty years. But the small Bonelli's eagle and the forbiciazze (fork-tailed kites) are still there. The golden eagle has returned, on the other hand, to the mountain par excellence, Etna, or jebel (mount), as the Arabs called it, as though it were the only mountain in Sicily.

Orazio Nicoloso is not an Etna guide but he has trained many. He may be the man who knows the volcano best. Having climbed the mountain on foot together, we waited for dawn in a recess in the central crater, heated by boiling lava from a few feet down. We told each other stories about Etna and chatted about the locals, who do not see the volcano as a devil but rather as a strict father. Finally, we turned from the crater to watch the sun rise in the clean, transparent air. The shadow of Etna was projected right across Sicily with its tip stretching to some imprecise point between Palermo and Trapani.

This immense volcano began its life over half a million years ago when there was originally just a large gulf in its place. The lava began to flow under the sea until Etna itself appeared, growing higher with each eruption. The Siculi considered Etna a god whom they called Adranon. They built and dedicated a temple to him surrounded by enormous forests and watched over by a thousand sacred dogs that savaged those with bad intentions but escorted the faithful. Some say that the dogs were Cirnecos – small, elegant Sicilian hunting dogs like greyhounds – with pointed ears and similar to the "Pharoah's dogs" probably imported from Africa by Phoenician merchants who traded with the Siculian cities on the banks of the Simeto river. Sicilian Greeks showed the Cirnecos on their coins, and they were the only dogs that Moslems would touch as they considered all others impure. Their skill in the hunt over the sharp sciare (cold lava flows) induced the peasants of Etna to keep this breed pure for centuries.

But there are other animals that are also typically Sicilian, such as the strong and agile Sanfratellano horse or the modicani cattle that are enclosed by muretti a siccari (dry walls) in the shade of immense carob trees, true monuments of nature. The carob is the best representation of the Sicilian peasant. It has firm, solid roots able to ensure survival in dry and rocky ground, huge thick evergreen leaves that give shade and cool in the torrid Sicilian heat, and poor quality fruit that is used to brighten stalls on festival days.

It is a strong and generous tree.

523 The extraordinary gorge of the Alcantara river on the border between the provinces of Catania and Messina was gouged out of an ancient lava bed.

The gradual erosion has revented the petrographic structure of the rock known as "columnar basalt," formed by prisms of rock modelled by the river.

THE SYMBOLIC PLANTS OF SICILY

*524, 525 and 528-529
These pictures show the
harvesting of the plants that
are considered the symbols of
the island – vines, olives and
oranges – yet all of them were
originally imported in
various epochs by different
colonists and invaders.
The most recent were the
prickly pear and the aloe,
which were imported by the
Spanish after the conquest of
America. Native plants and
trees include the birch, the
beech, dwarf palms, the carob
and fir trees. In certain
inland mountain villages –
like the snow-covered one
on the following pages –
the temperature is cool
enough to allow these
northern trees to survive.*

*526-527 A typical Sicilian
scene; a farmer and his
donkey on rocky ground,
where the prickly pear and
flowers flourish.*

ETNA
A STRICT FATHER

530 and 531 Etna is not considered to be a destroyer by the people that live on the slopes but rather a strict father. It was here that many European travelers visiting Sicily in the 18th and 19th centuries began to understand the sense of the quiet contrasts that characterize the island. The German, Johann Heinrich Bartels, noted how "the most delicate vegetation grows on blocks of spent fire." This immense volcano began life over half a million years ago when there was only a wide gulf in its place. The lava started to pour out from under the sea until, eruption after eruption, Etna emerged and continued to rise. The Siculi, some of the island's first inhabitants, considered the volcano to be a god whom they named Adranon, the lord of fire and war, and dedicated a temple to him surrounded by enormous forests and protected by a thousand sacred dogs.

532, 533 and 534-535
These pictures show both the destructive power of the lava and the faith of the people. Some eruptions are considered to have been stopped after processions were held of simulacra or the reliquaries of saints, such as the veil of St. Agatha, the patron saint of Catania. More recently, Etna has been the object of study by scientific researchers and by the Civil defense, seeking ways of diverting or stopping lava flows. In 1983, the world's first experiment to divert a lava flow was carried out (although attempts had been made since 1669 by ardimentosi brave men armed with picks and clubs) and in 1992, Professor Franco Barberi, President of the National Group of Volcanologists, successfully concluded "Operation Thrombosis," in which lava flows were encouraged to flow from high altitude caves down the same paths as flows from previous months. But Etna is also a laboratory of natural history, covered with plants up to a certain altitude, then home to the "holy thornbush" shown on the following pages.

PROTAGONISTS
IN THE FESTIVALS

The great popular tradition of the Baroque in Sicily might be thought to derive from the inherent theatricality of the style in that it is able to satisfy the ambition of peoples who wish to be protagonists after so many invasions and subjugations. Protagonism is one of the less obvious, but strong, qualities of Sicilians – whether it is a good or bad point depends on your point of view. Bartels noted it when he wrote his version of the observation made by the Syracusan Saverio Landolina Nava, "the enthusiasm of these men for festivals turns them into madmen, seeing that they have no opportunity for being heroes." Such an opportunity arises with the colossal effort required to carry the statue of St. Philip Syriac at breakneck speed down the slope towards Calatabiano or when the litter of St. Agatha is pulled up the steep San Giuliano hill in Catania, which is the slope of a volcano that has been extinct for centuries. These are collective efforts; where protagonism is really evident is in the festival of Sant'Alfio di Trecastagni.

The night of May 9th is filled with the agonizing cries of the nudi (men wearing just a pair of breeches and a red sash around their chest and women dressed but shoeless) who carry the giant candles on litters on their shoulders to the cathedral dedicated to the "three innocent lambs" (the saint actually had two brothers, Filadelfo and Cirino, who were martyred with him in a dungeon at Militello, though the eager crowd is there just for Alfio). This spring festival in the province of Catania was so important that in the 18th century women used to insert clauses in their marriage contract obliging their husbands to accompany them to it each year. It was also an opportunity to buy garlic, straw hats, tambourines and, more recently, watch the parade of Sicilian carts decorated with heroic scenes of the paladins of France, as described by story-tellers. Like in so many other festivals, the culmination of Sant'Alfio was i giochi di fuoco (a spectacle using fire). There are all types of such spectacles in Sicilian festivals; for example, the ones similar to those at Marina di Palermo enthusiastically described by Houel as "an enchanted wood prepared for the triumph of Amphitrite," and others less extinct. These pyrotechnical spectacles replaced the mosaici di fuoco (fire mosaics) like the one still to be seen at the festival of San Giacomo at

Caltagirone on the steps of the church of Santa Maria del Monte, and large ritual bonfires like the one on which King Burlone is burned at the end of the carnival in Acireale each year. This is thought to be Sicily's most beautiful carnival festival, with its gigantic allegorical floats, masked groups, bands that parade in a splendid Baroque setting, and the huge crowds equalled only by those at Sciacca during its carnival. Nevertheless, both the tradition of burning King Burlone and that of the papier-maché floats are relatively recent. The only "giants" used to be Mata and Grifone, the mythical founders of Messina whose floats tour the city on August 15th. More akin to an allegorical float was the Varca, a boat without a bottom made from papier maché on which men dressed as sailors toured the streets "fishing" for sausages, pork jelly, macaroni and wine in an amusing "alms collection." Ancient carnivals centered around the figure of "Nannu," a puppet of an old man whose death was ritually announced by the vecchia di li fusa (the old woman with the spindle), a remembrance of the myth of the three Fates. After the excess of Carnival, an entertaining outlet for an extremely rigid society, huge tables were laid, carnascialate (carnival jokes) were played in which barons and doctors (called Pisciacalamari) were made fun of and, in Catania, the dirittu di li 'ntuppateddi allowed women, when masked, all sorts of liberties. "Nannu" died to the wails of the hired mourners but always with the certainty of rising again the following year, like in ancient myths. This is recalled in a verse of the repitu (the chorus of two voices in the hired mourners): "Morsi lu Nannu, lu nannu muriu. Ppi' 'nautru annu nun pipita cchiu." (Nannu is dead, Nannu has died. He will not return for another year). Before dying, King Burlone had made a will, usually rather obscene, reporting all the sins of the people which he would take with him in his role as a scapegoat.

The most authentic modern-day version of Carnival in Sicily is certainly that of the Mastru di campu (Master of the Field) at Mezzojuso, a parody of the siege of Solunto Castle, where Queen Blanche of Navarre, the widow of King Martin and the deputy ruler of the kingdom, had taken refuge from Count Bernardo Cabrera whose love for Blanche was unrequited.

The festival, which much resembles the spirit of the Opera dei Pupi (Puppet Theater), has three characters: the King, the Queen and the Master (also called the General, who is tall, lanky and wears a red mask). A tubbiana (troop of masked characters) made up of devils, wizards, peasants, shepherds, ministers and cuirassiers on horseback, all in 15th-century Spanish costume, surrounds the main characters. The King, the Queen and their ministers take their places on the platform of the castle, then the Master arrives on horseback to a drum roll, surrounded by soldiers and barons. He makes signs that show he is in love with the Queen. He then sends his declaration of war to the King and the battle begins: with his sword unsheathed he attacks with theatrical gestures one, two, three times but the King wounds him in a duel forcing him into a theatrical caruta (fall) from the castle walls as the Queen faints. But the Master, restored to life, takes command of his troops again, the cannons fire and he succeeds in scaling the castle walls to reach the Queen and declare his love. Chased away once more, he turns to craftiness. He bribes the enemy soldiers, captures the King and, arm in arm, he parades with the Queen to the sound of music, dances and nursery rhymes: "Purra, purra papirribbella. Bichiri, bichiri, papirribbella." It is very reminiscent of traditional Carnival when Pulcinella plays tarantellas and fasolas on his lute with other masked characters with friscaletti, viulini, scattagnetti, tammurini e tammureddi, e corni e brogne (whistles, violins, tambourines and tambourels, and horns and shells) like in the banni d'è mascariati (bands) which still exist in Sicily. There are the band of Umbrillara from Santa Teresa di Riva in the province of Messina and the shabby band from the Villaggio Santa Maria Goretti, the most popular in Catania, which plays march tunes during the rugby matches of the Amatori rugby team. The latter shows the best side of a city raised on the enjoyment of thumbing its rose at others and realizing dreams from nothing.

The pecchi (the names of these musical players) are as carnivalesque as any Sicilian masked character: Pecura janca, Cacaniuru, Sasizza and Furmagginu against Tofalu, Nofiu Taddarita and, of course, Peppi 'Nnappa, the most lovable character also because he is so well known by spectators of the Opera dei Pupi.

After Carnival comes Easter which is maybe the largest of all festivals in Sicily. It is filled with contrasting features; for example, the Devil is part of the procession in Prizzi in the province of Palermo. A medieval legend tells of a group of demons that invaded the village and encouraged the inhabitants to sin and for centuries now, the abballu di li diavuli (the dance of the devils) has been relived during Holy Week; young men dressed in red outfits, large red masks and goatskins that drape down over their shoulders tour the streets looking for victims from whom they can demand money for something to drink. Death tours with them dressed in a yellow outfit and mask and armed with a loaded crossbow.

Devils and Death in yellow are also to be seen in Adrano in the province of Catania, where since the 18th century, they have been the main characters in a holy play which is performed on Easter Day between the Norman castle and the church. The plot is simple and even trivial: the forces of evil – Lucifer, Ashtaroth, Beelzebub and Death – want to possess Humanity but Archangel Michael intervenes and frees them. Humanity and Michael are impersonated by children who wear white clothes while the devils are dressed in black, monstrous outfits. Even more ugly is Death who, realizing that he will not be able to vanquish Humanity, breaks his arrow and throws it into the crowd. The people all scrabble for the parts, which are considered to be lucky charms.

Demons are also an element at San Fratello, where the streets are filled with "Jews" on the Wednesday and Friday of Holy Week. Like the devils in Prizzi, the Jews are allowed to do pretty much as they like; it seems that in the past, armed with swords, trumpets and discipline (whips), these "Jews" actually perpetrated vendettas.

There are also mystical spectacles that originated from medieval laudi (hymns of praise) lyrical in the beginning but later transformed into dramatic modes. Lodate (praises) and lamenti (laments) are one of the rare polyphonic works of the Sicilian oral tradition sung by the male choirs of various monastic confraternities. The lyrics are taken from episodes of the Gospels and are mainly in Sicilian dialect though some are in Italian or a rough liturgical Latin; they deal with the death and resurrection of Christ. Out of these lyrical dramas, groups representing Martyrs, Mysteries, Casazzas and Devotions have evolved.

539 The deeds of Orlando,
Rinaldo, Angelica and
Emperor Charlemagne made
a great impression at
a time when cinema and
television did not exist and
the theaters were almost

exclusively the privilege
of the rich. Today, the great
families of puppet masters
have almost all disappeared
with the exception of the
Cuticchio in Palermo and the
Napoli in Catania.

Processions of the Mysteries, (a group of sculptures inspired by the Gospel), parade at Trapani, Marsala, Caltanissetta and Enna. At Enna, the hooded confradias (confraternities) march to the rhythm of the tabbala, a huge drum, while at Caltanissetta ten musical bands each perform a funeral march on the Thursday before Easter, disturbed by troccule (wooden boards which youngsters strike). On Easter Day, the bands perform lively marches at the lu 'ncontru (meeting) between the statues of the Grieving and the Risen Christ. This is the most joyful moment of the festival because the Savior is not really the protagonist in this festival. As Sciascia wrote, "… he had died … but his mother was still alive: grieving, enclosed in her black mantle of heavy grief … The true drama was hers: earthly, physical." This is confirmed by the dialogue given by Favara between Mary and the blacksmith who is making the preparations for the crucifixion, wracked by grief. The people therefore feel close to the role played in the divine sacrifice of the Madonna to such a point that, in the poignant presentation at Burgio, she becomes the unquestioned protagonist of the drama.

On Easter Day, the people rejoice for Mary when the gigantic figure of St. Peter tours the streets of the "Giunta" in Caltagirone in search of the Virgin to announce the Resurrection. He then hurries to meet the Risen Christ, who stands between two Jews, called Chicchittu and Nancittu by the people. The joyful pealing of bells is mixed with the equally spirited trills of the terracotta friscaletti (whistles), the humble toy of Sicilian children, sold on the festival stalls at Easter.

THE CARTS
OF THE PALADINS

540 and 541 The exploits of
the paladins of France are
relived on the sides of
traditional Sicilian carts even
if they are kept in museums
like that of Aci Sant'Antonio
in the province of Catania.
Occasionally they are
paraded in public, as happens
at the festival of Sant'Alfio in
Trecastagni.

THE BATTLE
OF THE MASTER
OF THE FIELD

542 and 543 Epic themes are the subject of the pantomime *Mastru di campu* (Master of the Field) in Mezzojuso in the province of Palermo. This performance is perhaps the most authentic of popular Sicilian carnivals. The show parodies the siege of the castle of Solunto where Queen Blanche of Navarre (widow of King Martin and deputy head of the country) had hidden from the Count of Modica, Bernardo Cabrera. A troop of masked characters, typical of carnivals from the past, moves around the main characters of the pantomime: the Master of the Field (who succeeds in taking the castle after bribing the guards), the King and the Queen.

CARNIVAL TIME
AT ACIREALE

544, 545 and 546-547
"The best Carnival in Sicily," with allegorical papier-maché floats, vehicles covered with flowers and figures made using oranges and other citrus fruits, is by definition the Carnival at Acireale, which attracts a huge number of visitors each year. The lovely Baroque city is literally invaded by tourists who often take advantage of the visit for a "health holiday," spending the morning in the spa and the afternoon to late evening in the streets watching the parades of floats, masked groups and lively musical bands. A similar festival takes place in Sciacca near Agrigento but the tradition of allegorical floats and that of burning King Burlone at the end of the event are relatively recent. The personification of the ancient Sicilian carnival is "Nannu," a puppet that dies as a scapegoat after having taken on the collective sins of the people.

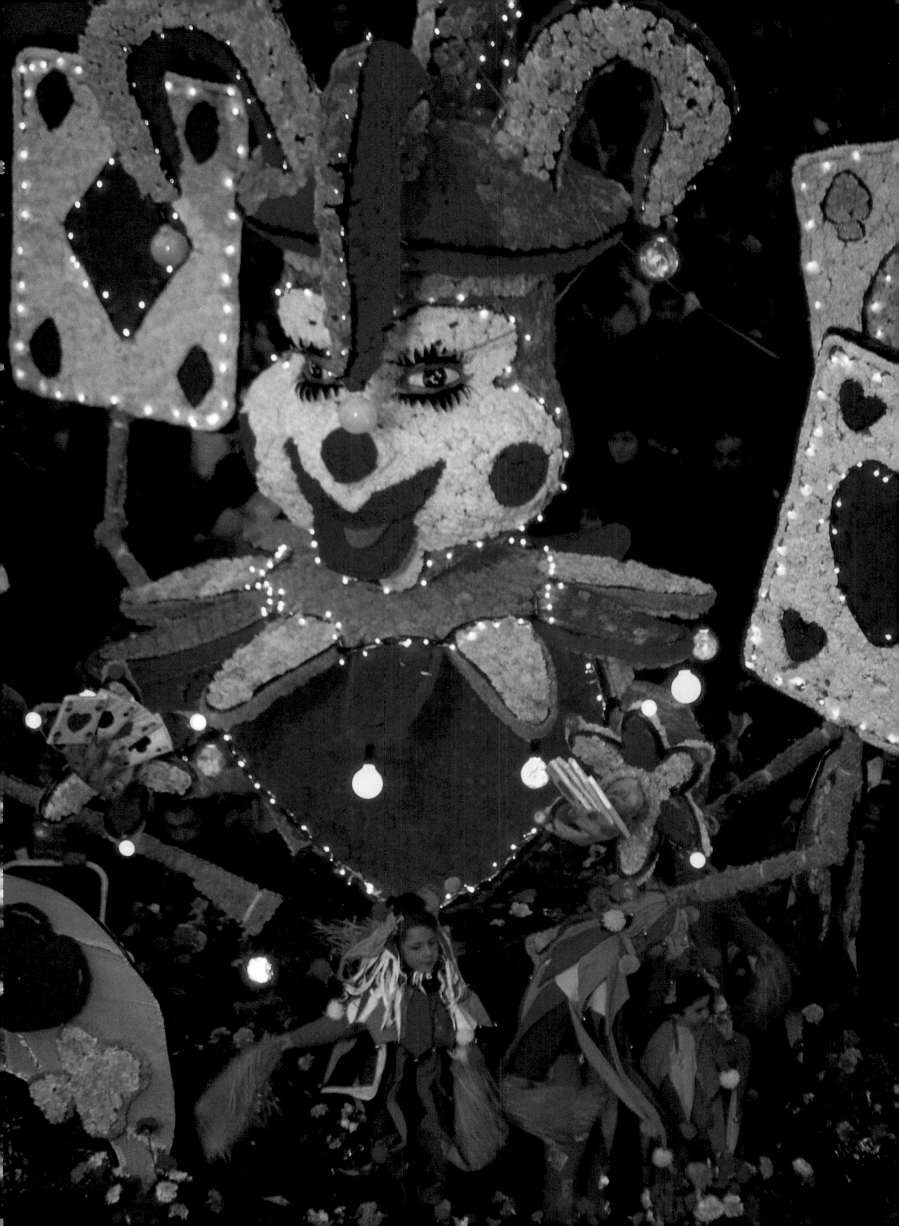

THE DEVIL
BEHIND
THE ALTAR

*548 and 549 Devils are the
main characters in the Easter
celebration at Adrano in
Catania. This takes place in
the main square below the
Norman castle. The plot of
the "Diavolata" is simple and
even trivial: the forces of evil
represented by Lucifer,
Ashtaroth, Beelzebub and
Death (this last in yellow)
attempt to take possession
of Humanity after the death
of Christ – but with the
Resurrection, Archangel
Michael frees Humanity.*

THE CONFRATERNITIES OF ENNA

550 and 551 The Good
Friday procession in Enna is
special because of the many
confradies (confraternities)
that parade in hoods.
The procession marches to
the rhythm of the tabbala
(large drum). During the
procession the Black
Madonna of Enna is
devotedly carried on the
shoulders of the faithful.

THE DAYS
OF THE JEWS

552 and 553 San Fratello is a village in the Nebrodi hills where the inhabitants speak a strange Gallic-Italian dialect. Holy Week here is characterized by the presence of "Jews" who wear red hoods and jackets and carry swords, whips and tinplate trumpets. They are allowed to do whatever they like on the Wednesday and Friday before Easter. The same happens at Prizzi in the province of Palermo where the Abballu di li diavuli (Dance of the Devils) is relived each year. Young men in red outfits and masks and wearing a goatskin over their shoulders tour the streets in search of "victims" forced to give them money to spend on drink.

A SPANISH EASTER

554 and 555 Night-time pictures taken of Holy Week in Caltanissetta, one of the loveliest celebrations on the island. These cerimonies had their origin in medieval hymns of praise that were turned from lyric into dramatic and which were strongly promoted during the period of the Spanish domination. "Martyrs," "Mysteries," "Casazzas" and "Devotions" came into being; they still survive in many other towns in Sicily.

"LI SCHETTI"
OF CALATAFIMI

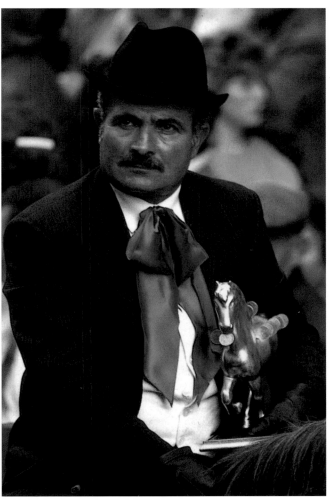

*556, 557 and 558-559 One of
the most curious popular
festivals in Sicily is the
Festival of the Crucifix in
Calatafimi, the small town in
the province of Agrigento
known mostly for the Battle
of May 15, 1860, won by
Garibaldi against, the
Bourbon troops. The festival,
also known as "di li schetti,"
has a parade of men dressed
in black carrying rifles. The*
*parade undoubtedly extols
the "heroic" component of
Sicilian festivals that was
highlighted in the 19th
century by the German
Johann Heinrich Bartels
when, in contemplation of the
Syracusan Saverio Landolina,
he wrote, "the enthusiasm of
these men for festivals turns
them into madmen, seeing
that they have no opportunity
for being heroes."*